Classroom Discourse and Teacher Development

D1375762

CUSTOMER SERVICE EXCELLENCE

Edge Hill University

Learning Services

Edge Hill University
LEARNING SERVICES

Renew Online: http://library.edgehill.ac.uk

24/7 telephone renewals: 01695 58 4333

Help line: 01695 58 4286

Edinburgh Textbooks in Applied Linguistics

Visit the Edinburgh Textbooks in Applied Linguistics website at
www.euppublishing.com/series/eual

Classroom Discourse and Teacher Development

Steve Walsh

EDINBURGH
University Press

© Steve Walsh, 2013

Edinburgh University Press Ltd
22 George Square, Edinburgh EH8 9LF

www.euppublishing.com

Typeset in Adobi Garamond
by Norman Tilley Graphics Ltd, Northampton
and printed and bound in Great Britain
by CPI Group (UK) Ltd, Croydon CR0 4YY

A CIP record for this book is available from the British Library

ISBN 978 0 7486 4518 3 (hardback)
ISBN 978 0 7486 4517 6 (paperback)
ISBN 978 0 7486 4519 0 (webready PDF)
ISBN 978 0 7486 7784 9 (epub)

The right of Steve Walsh
to be identified as author of this work
has been asserted in accordance with
the Copyright, Designs and Patents Act 1988.

Contents

Series Editors' Preface

This series of single-author volumes published by Edinburgh University Press takes a contemporary view of applied linguistics. The intention is to make provision for the wide range of interests in contemporary applied linguistics which are provided for at the Master's level.

The expansion of Master's postgraduate courses in recent years has had two effects:

1. What began almost half a century ago as a wholly cross-disciplinary subject has found a measure of coherence so that now most training courses in Applied Linguistics have similar core content.
2. At the same time the range of specialisms has grown, as in any developing discipline. Training courses (and professional needs) vary in the extent to which these specialisms are included and taught.

Some volumes in the series will address the first development noted above, while the others will explore the second. It is hoped that the series as a whole will provide students beginning postgraduate courses in Applied Linguistics, as well as language teachers and other professionals wishing to become acquainted with the subject, with a sufficient introduction for them to develop their own thinking in applied linguistics and to build further into specialist areas of their own choosing.

The view taken of applied linguistics in the Edinburgh Textbooks in Applied Linguistics Series is that of a theorising approach to practical experience in the language professions, notably, but not exclusively, those concerned with language learning and teaching. It is concerned with the problems, the processes, the mechanisms and the purposes of language in use.

Like any other applied discipline, applied linguistics draws on theories from related disciplines with which it explores the professional experience of its practitioners and which in turn are themselves illuminated by that experience. This two-way relationship between theory and practice is what we mean by a theorising discipline.

The volumes in the series are all premised on this view of Applied Linguistics as a theorising discipline which is developing its own coherence. At the same time, in order to present as complete a contemporary view of applied linguistics as possible other approaches will occasionally be expressed.

Each volume presents its author's own view of the state of the art in his or her topic. Volumes will be similar in length and in format, and, as is usual in a textbook series, each will contain exercise material for use in class or in private study.

Alan Davies
W. Keith Mitchell

List of Abbreviations

CA	conversation analysis
CIC	classroom interactional competence
CLCA	corpus linguistics and conversation analysis
CCDA	critical classroom discourse analysis
CL	corpus linguistics
CMC	computer mediated communication
DA	discourse analysis
IC	interactional competence
IRF	initiation, response, feedback
RP	reflective practice
SETT	self-evaluation of teacher talk
SLA	second language acquisition
ZPD	zone of proximal development

Chapter 1

Introduction

In this chapter, the case is made for putting an understanding of classroom discourse at the centre of any second language teacher education programme, whether it is a formal programme under the guidance of a teacher educator or a more informal, self-directed programme of teacher development. It is argued that in order to improve their professional practice, language teachers need to gain a detailed, up-close understanding of their local context by focusing on the complex relationship between teacher language, classroom interaction and learning. In order to do this, I suggest, there is a need to revisit and reconceptualise the notion of reflective practice by giving teachers appropriate tools which allow them to reflect on and improve their professional practice.

In this first chapter, the aim is to sketch out the landscape of the book by describing and critiquing its key components, each of which is developed in the sections below:

1. In section 1, the notion of teachers as researchers is both described and analysed from the perspectives of action research and reflective practice (RP). A critique is offered of the place of RP in second language teacher education, and the case is made for a revitalisation and reconfiguration of RP.
2. Section 2 offers a theoretical perspective, outlining the importance of socio-cultural theories of learning to second language teacher education and development.
3. In section 3, as the backdrop to the present book, I offer a critique of studies which have placed classroom interaction at the centre of teacher development and consider future directions.
4. The next section provides a perspective on future challenges for learners and teachers from the position of classroom interaction, learning and professional development.
5. Finally, an overview of the book is presented.

1.1 TEACHERS AS RESEARCHERS

Under the notion of second language teacher *education*, as distinct from second language teacher *training* (Richards and Nunan 1990; Wallace 1991; Edge 2001), the focus of attention is on the need to enable teachers to develop themselves. There is clearly more to teacher preparation than skills training; teachers need to be equipped with the tools that will enable them to find out about their own classrooms and make adjustments (Bartlett 1990). In short, teachers must learn to change their role from teacher to teacher-researcher, a logical extension of what Wallace terms 'the applied science model' (1991: 8) of teacher education, first proposed by the American sociologist Donald Schön (1983, 1996). Schön put forward a model of *reflection in action* under which teachers and teachers in training are involved in critical thought, questioning and re-appraising their actions in the second language classroom (1983). More recently, there has been a call for the concept of *reflection in action* to be re-interpreted as 'reflection after action' (Eraut 1995), since teachers cannot reflect as they teach; instead, a cycle of action-reflection-further action is preferred, with a slight distancing between each of the stages.

One of the central arguments of this book is that reflective practice in the fields of applied linguistics, TESOL and education has become an accepted and respected professional activity without a corresponding data-led description of its value, processes and impact. Essentially, while RP is now a key element of almost any teacher education programme, recognised for its value and significance, it has also, arguably, become a tired and overused institutional requirement. Although it is regarded as a crucial element of most teacher development programmes (Clarke and Otaky 2006), there is evidence to suggest that many teachers (and teacher educators) do not know how to reflect, nor are they, in most cases, taught *how* to reflect. The consequence according to Grushka et al. is that teachers produce 'metacognitive rambles … focused on minor technical aspects of their teaching' (2006: 239). One of the key issues to be addressed in this book is the extent to which RP, seen as being central to teacher education and development and advocated by many professionals (including myself), can be refocused by getting practitioners to place classroom inter-action at the centre of their reflections.

Recent attempts to critique RP (see, for example, Borg 2002; Akbari 2007) show it in a rather negative light, regarded as something of a luxury, and even viewed as irrelevant. For busy professionals, RP is not given space or priority, leading many to become members of a community of 'disbelievers' who are highly critical of the notion (cf. Hobbs 2007). There is a strong sense that for many in the field, RP is seen more as an institutional requirement which prioritises its written form over a spoken version. McCabe et al. (2011), for example, found that many student-teachers on initial teacher education programmes benefited more from discussions about their teaching with peers and teacher educators than they did from completing written report forms. Murphy (2012) calls for a move towards a more 'dialogic' approach to reflective practice, while Walsh (2011) considers the role of teacher educators in 'shaping' the reflections of teachers through spoken feedback.

It is fair to say, then, that there is some consensus that there needs to be a refocus-ing of RP as both a written and spoken process. Some of these issues were given an airing at a recent BAAL/CUP conference (Spiro and Wickens 2011); one of the papers (Mann and Walsh 2011) presented concerns about the predominance of written and institutional forms of reflection, arguing the need for reflective tools which can be tailored to specific contexts and facilitate detailed, up-close, 'ecological' (cf. van Lier 2000) professional understanding. This argument is developed in Chapter 6.

Despite these rather critical observations, one of the main arguments of this book is that RP is both positive, necessary and key to teacher development, but that it needs to be refocused if it is to survive. For teachers to become researchers of their own practice, I will argue, they need appropriate tools, data and dialogue with other or more experienced professionals. Central features to be explored in the book are, therefore: the need for RP to be taught on pre-service teacher education programmes; the desirability for more appropriate tools to facilitate reflection; the importance of recognising that RP should be evidence-based using data taken from classrooms; the need for RP to be removed from the constraints of institutional requirements so that it might become a career-long practice; the value of dialogic rather than written forms of reflection. In addition, the whole notion of 'teacher as researcher' will be revisited and reconfigured to incorporate some of the key principles of action research and by re-evaluating what is meant by 'data'.

Currently, and in most contexts where RP is practised, teachers adopt a retrospective stance and reflect on past actions in an endeavour to increase their understanding of the teaching/learning process (Wallace 1998). Competencies are acquired through and by the participants who have an active role in their own development, which in turn is based on two types of knowledge: *received knowledge*, 'the intellectual content of the profession' (Wallace 1991: 14), including the specific knowledge (linguistic and pedagogic) that language teachers need in order to perform their role; and *experiential knowledge*, based on the experience gained in the classroom and reflection on that experience. To use Wallace's terms, experiential knowledge is based on knowledge-in-action plus reflection on that knowledge. Mann makes a similar distinction: 'Received knowledge is the stuff of dictionaries and is more verifiable. Experiential knowledge is not a matter of fact, but a complex mix of feeling, thought and individual perspective' (2001: 58). Clearly, both types of knowledge are important, but it is the second which is of most concern here since it rests on the assumption that teachers can and should reflect on their practices and learn from them. Central to the notion of experiential knowledge is collaborative discussion, where thoughts and ideas about classroom practice are articulated. Put simply, reflection on practice does not occur in isolation, but in discussion with another practitioner, a form of cooperative development, involving a 'Speaker' and an 'Understander', whose role is to enhance professional understanding through dialogue (Edge 1992, 2001).

The logical extension of reflective practice is for teachers to identify and address problems which are specific to their own context, a central concern of action research, which rests on the premise that teachers can and should investigate their own classrooms (Cohen et al. 2011). The starting point is the identification of a problem; the process continues with data collection and analysis, and finally outcomes are suggested. The value and relevance of action research are self-evident: helping teachers to focus on problems in their own classrooms and to identify solutions is desirable from the position of both professional development and student learning. As Johnson puts it: 'The more research-driven knowledge teachers have, the better their teaching performances will be' (1995: 29; see also Johnson 2009). Under this view, 'research-driven knowledge' is data-led and, more importantly, based on data derived from a teacher's own classroom. According to Nunan (1989: 3), there are a number of reasons why teachers might be interested in researching their own classrooms. Firstly, because teachers have to justify educational innovations; secondly, because teachers are constantly involved in intellectual and social change; thirdly, because becoming a teacher-researcher is a logical stage in the process of professional self-development. From the perspective of this book, then, I am suggesting that teachers' ability to collect and analyse data (derived from classroom interaction) is central to their professional development.

Because teacher-researchers are both the producers and consumers of their research (Kumaravadivelu 1999), since they both own the data and are responsible for effecting changes to classroom practices, the process is more private and, arguably, less intimidating. The concern is to enhance understanding of local context rather than generalise to a broader one, though this may also occur. Following Wallace (1998, above), developing understandings of local context lies at the heart of this book and is, I suggest, central to both professional development and enhanced learning. There are at least three conditions needed for understandings of local context to occur:

- Condition 1: the research takes place in the classroom.
- Condition 2: teacher-researchers reflect and act on what they observe.
- Condition 3: understandings emerge through dialogue.

1.1.1 Research takes place in the classroom

According to Nunan, much of the research that goes on in second language teaching is deemed irrelevant, resulting in a 'wedge between researcher and practitioner'. One of the reasons is that teachers' voices are often unheard, replaced by the researcher's perspective; another is that much research is still conducted under experimental conditions in classrooms created for research purposes (Nunan 1996: 42). This startling revelation suggests an urgent need for research that is located in 'ordinary' classrooms, conducted by teachers for their own ends; understanding and professional development can only be enhanced when the process of inquiry is carried out *in situ*, in the teacher's natural environment. Van Lier terms this 'ecological research':

> Ecological research pays a great deal of attention to the smallest detail of the interaction, since within these details may be contained the seeds of learning. The reflective teacher can learn to 'read' the environment to notice such details. An organism 'resonates' with its environment, picking up affordances in its activities. This is a different level of understanding than the one based in explicit knowledge or studied facts. It is a deeper sense of reflection in action. (2000: 11)

The main attraction of this view of 'reflection in action' is that teachers work very closely with the data they collect in their own context, their own 'environment', to use van Lier's word. The understanding they gain from working with the detail of their data is very much their own – personal, private and internal – enabling teachers to read the interactional processes and interactive signals as they arise. Public owner-ship does not come into question, neither does generalisability; research is a process of inquiry, conducted by the teacher for the teacher. Other researchers have called for class-based research which is conducted in the teacher's own classroom, preferably by the teacher (see, for example, Bailey and Nunan 1996; Wallace 1998). One of the main advantages of action research is that there is a unification of theory and practice since the smallest details can be studied, changes implemented and then evaluated (van Lier 2000). The main reason for the potential for such microscopic analysis is the fact that the research is located in a context which is both clearly defined and familiar to the teacher-researcher.

1.1.2 Teacher-researchers reflect and act on what they observe

The second condition is very much in tune with the broad philosophy of action research: research plus action, not just research for research's sake (Cohen et al. 2011); when participants 'do something' based on their self-observation, the ultimate bene-factors will be their students. In the words of Kemmis and McTaggart:

> Action research involves problem-posing, not just problem-solving. It does not start from a view of 'problems' as pathologies. It is motivated by a quest to improve and understand the world by changing it and learning how to improve it from the effects of the changes made. (1992: 21–2)

The suggestion here is that the very act of 'posing problems' and coming to under-stand them is, in itself, developmental. Problems may or may not be solved; the real value lies in discussing options and considering possibilities, a process of 'exploratory practice' (Allwright and Lenzuen 1997). Reflection and action result in a kind of 'emergent understanding', an ongoing process of enhanced awareness.

For most second language teachers, this vision of class-based research might appear somewhat daunting – teachers are not automatically equipped with classroom obser-vation skills and may know even less about how to process and analyse data (Nunan 1991). Not only are L2 teachers normally too busy to take on such a commitment, most have not been trained in class-based research techniques. Furthermore, if action research is regarded as something that is imposed, it loses its 'emancipatory' (Zuber-Skerritt 1996) or 'empowering' function (Wallace 1998). In other words, the research has to be carried out following a teacher's *desire* to learn more about a particular aspect of their professional life. Teachers have to have ownership of their research and through collaborative dialogue take actions which they deem appropriate. As described elsewhere in the literature (see, for example, Winter 1996), teacher action is based on self-evaluation, contributing to professional development in the vein of what has been termed 'practical action research' (Grundy 1987: 154).

1.1.3 Understanding requires dialogue

Action research has always been regarded as a collaborative process involving dialogue (Walsh 2011; Winter 1996; Zuber-Skerritt 1996). Dialogue is a crucial part of the reflection-action-further action cycle, since it allows for clarification, questioning and ultimately enhanced understanding. Conversation is the means by which new ideas are expressed, doubts aired and concerns raised (Wells 1999). Extending a socio-cultural view of learning to teacher education (Lantolf and Thorne 2006), it becomes very quickly apparent that professional development occurs through dialogue. Dialogue can establish 'proximal processes' or contexts which create opportunities for learning potential (Bruner 1990). There are parallels here in the place of 'dialogic teaching' advocated by mainstream education practitioners and researchers (see, for example, Alexander 2008; Mortimer and Scott 2003; Mercer 2005). Essentially, the argument advocated by this group of researchers is that, through dialogue and dis-cussion, children learn to think and develop together. Based on sociocultural theories of learning and development, where learning is mediated by language, the central claim of researchers like Robin Alexander and Neil Mercer is that learning occurs primarily through dialogue. I am making the same argument in a teacher education setting.

In a teacher education/development context, and from a sociocultural perspective, teachers are 'scaffolded' through their 'zones of proximal development' (ZPD) to a higher plane of understanding through the dialogues they have with other professionals (van Lier 1996). Under this perspective, reflection and action alone are insufficient means of allowing professional development – scaffolded dialogues, where issues are clarified and new levels of understanding attained, are central to reflective practice. A fuller discussion on the place of sociocultural theories of learning in second language teacher development is taken up in the next section.

1.2 L2 TEACHER EDUCATION AND SOCIOCULTURAL THEORY

Sociocultural theories of learning emphasise its social nature, which takes place as learners interact with the 'expert knower' 'in a context of social interactions leading to understanding' (Röhler and Cantlon 1996: 2). Under this view, learners collec-tively and actively construct their own knowledge and understanding by making connections, building mental schemata and concepts through collaborative meaning making.

In addition to the social nature of learning, sociocultural theory emphasises the fact that the mind is *mediated*. In his sociocultural theory of mind, Vygotsky (1978, 1986, 1999) maintains that human beings make use of symbolic tools, such as language, to both interpret and regulate the world we live in and our relationships with each other. Lantolf explains mediation as follows: 'we use symbolic tools or signs to mediate and regulate our relationships with others and with ourselves and thus change the nature of these relationships' (2000: 1). Our relationship with the world is an indirect, or *mediated*, one, which is established through the use of symbolic tools. (Lantolf 2000; Lantolf and Thorne 2006). Understanding the ways in which human social and mental activity are organised through symbolic tools is the role of psychology, under a Vygotskyan perspective. While thought and speech are separate, they are 'tightly interrelated in a dialectic unity in which publicly derived speech completes privately initiated thought' (Lantolf 2000: 7). In other words, understanding and knowledge are 'publicly derived' but privately internalised. Language, under Vygotskyan theory, is 'a means for engaging in social and cognitive activity' (Ahmed 1994: 158). From a teacher education perspective, we can easily extend these ideas to demonstrate how teachers first gain new knowledge, new ideas or new understandings through interacting with colleagues or educators. This 'publicly derived' new knowledge is then privately internalised as the same teachers take ownership and apply new practices to their own context. The process is both dialectic and dialogic: it entails dialogue with other professionals which then becomes a personal or individual practice.

Although it is important to remember that Vygotskyan theory was originally conceptualised in the L1 context and is directed at mother-tongue language development (Gillen 2000), it has considerable relevance to enhancing understandings of both SLA (second language acquisition) (see, for example, Lantolf and Appel 1994; Lantolf 2000; Lantolf and Thorne 2006) and teacher development (Johnson 2009). Here, I would like to develop some of the ideas put forward in the previous section and argue that a sociocultural theory of learning has much to offer in developing a more dialogic approach to teacher development.

The discussion begins with an outline of three key Vygotskyan principles:

1. The social nature of knowledge.
2. Learning takes place in the zone of proximal development.
3. Learning is assisted by scaffolding.

(Please note: in the discussion which follows, learning and development are regarded as being equivalent, while 'learners' are seen as either teachers following a structured teacher education programme, or teachers working on their own professional development.)

1.2.1 The social nature of knowledge

The dynamism of social interaction and its effects on development are central to Vygotsky's work. Unlike many other theories of self-development, or ontogenesis, which consider the individual as an enclosed unit, Vygotsky stresses the importance of social interaction to an individual's development: 'In this view, the "dynamic edge" of development consists of interactive processes that take place between the child and others' (Hickman 1990: 237).

Learning, in the first instance, is regarded as *interpsychological*, occurring between those members of society who have already mastered skills and knowledge and those who are in the process of acquiring them (e.g., a teacher and his learners, a teacher educator and her students). Learning, under this perspective, is defined as a social activity like others such as reading a book or listening to music – activities which have an inseparable social dimension whether performed alone or with others. According to one of Vygotsky's better-known followers, participation in even the simplest activity, such as reading a newspaper, is a socially constructed process (Leont'ev 1981). Learning a language too is regarded as a mental process which is inextricably linked to our social identity and relationships. But there is more to this argument: Leont'ev is making the point that whatever the object of our learning is, it is also socially constructed. So, for example, learning a language is socially constructed both as an activity (the learning process) and construct (the language). This is a perspective echoed in a different, linguistic context by Halliday (1978), who asserts that language itself is interwoven with social structure and system.

Sociocultural learning theory emphasises the social, dynamic and collaborative dimensions of learning; both Bruner (1983, 1990) and Vygotsky (1978, 1986, 1999) stress its 'transactional' nature, whereby learning occurs in the first instance through interaction with others, who are more experienced and in a position to guide and support the actions of the novice. During this part of the process, language is used as a 'symbolic tool' to clarify and make sense of new knowledge, with learners relying heavily on discussions with the 'expert knower'. As new ideas and knowledge are internalised, learners use language to comment on what they have learnt; oral communication is the 'organising function' (Hickman 1990: 236) used to both transmit and clarify new information and then to reflect on and rationalise what has been learnt – a gradual process of *self-regulation*, explained by Ahmed: 'a linguistically constituted mental process … through which the locus of control of mental activity shifts from the external context … to the internal mind' (1994: 158). In other words, cognitive development is realised when an individual's mental processing is independent of the external context; learning moves from the *interpsychological* to the *intrapsychological*. Essentially, new meanings are *appropriated*; that is, learners gain ownership and attach their own understanding. Throughout, language acts as a symbolic tool, mediating interpersonal and intrapersonal activity. This entire process occurs within the *zone of proximal development* (ZPD), the second of the principles presented here.

1.2.2 Learning takes place in the zone of proximal development

Vygotsky's original definition of the zone of proximal development (ZPD) is as follows:

> the zone of proximal development … is the distance between the actual development level as determined by independent problem solving and the level of potential development as determined by problem solving under adult guidance or in collaboration with more capable peers. (1978: 86)

According to Lantolf, rather than attaching spatial or temporal dimensions to the construct, the ZPD should be regarded as 'a metaphor for observing and understanding how mediated means are appropriated and internalized'. Lantolf goes on to offer his own definition of the ZPD: 'the collaborative construction of opportunities ... for individuals to develop their mental abilities' (2000: 17). A number of key terms emerge from the definitions of Vygotsky and Lantolf, including 'collaboration', 'construction', 'opportunities', 'development'. Other writers use a similar terminology: van Lier, for example, refers to opportunities for learning as 'affordances' (2000: 252), while Swain and Lapkin talk about 'occasions for learning' (1998: 320). As a construct in the present context, the value of the ZPD lies in its potential for enabling consideration of the 'give and take' in any teacher development process; that is, the ways in which – through dialogue – new understandings are acquired, developed and internalised. Throughout this book, therefore, the 'collaborative construction' of opportunities for learning is examined through the ways in which teachers collectively construct meaning through enhanced understandings of L2 classroom inter-action. The ZPD paradigm is welcomed for its inherent implication that any learning process can be broken down into a series of inter-related stages and that learners need to be helped to progress from one stage to the next through dialogue with others. It is the process of giving assistance or scaffolding which warrants more attention from a classroom discourse perspective; the discussion now turns to the third principle of the sociocultural theories considered in this section: scaffolding.

1.2.3 Learners are assisted by scaffolding

The term 'scaffolding' is used to refer to the linguistic support given to a learner. Support is given up to the point where a learner can 'internalise external knowledge and convert it into a tool for conscious control' (Bruner 1990: 25). Scaffolding is 'an instructional tool that reduces learning ambiguity' (Doyle 1986: 3). Central to the notion are the important polar concepts of challenge and support. Learners are led to an understanding of a task by, on the one hand, a teacher's provision of appropriate amounts of challenge to maintain interest and involvement, and, on the other, support to ensure understanding. Support typically involves segmentation and ritualisation so that learners have, in the first instance, limited choice in how they go about a task which is broken down into manageable component parts (Bruner 1990: 29). Once a task has been mastered, scaffolds are removed and the learner is left to reflect and comment on the task.

Clearly, the amount of scaffolded support given will depend very much on the perceived evaluation by the 'expert' of what is needed by the 'novice'. In a classroom context, where so much is happening at once, such fine judgements can be difficult to make. Deciding whether to intervene or withdraw in the moment by moment construction of classroom interaction requires great sensitivity and awareness on the part of the teacher and inevitably teachers do not 'get it right' every time. Similarly, in a teacher education context, teacher educators need to be sensitive regarding how much support to offer at any one time, especially in the feedback meetings which typically follow practice teaching (see Harris 2013).

Previous researchers have commented on the value of scaffolding in contexts where learners have an opportunity to express themselves and clarify what they want to say. As Martin puts it:

> A good conversation is neither a fight nor a contest. Circular in form, cooperative in manner and constructive in intent, it is an interchange of ideas by those who see themselves not as adversaries but as human beings come together to talk and listen and learn from each other. (1985: 3)

Conversation is the essence of all professional dialogue, the prime force through which meanings are negotiated, concepts explained and understood, exchanges of opinion given. Instructional conversations have been trialled in a number of contexts (see, for example, Goldenberg 1992). They are essentially discussion-based lessons in which linguistic and conceptual understanding of key areas are affected through teacher-led discussion based on student contributions. Instructional situations are highly complex, and for scaffolding to work learners need to be given opportunities to ask and answer questions according to Sternberg's principle of question and comment generation: 'The single most helpful thing a teacher can do is to take [learners'] questions and comments seriously and turn those questions and comments into learning opportunities' (1994: 137).

Thus far, the discussion has focused on the place of action research in second language teacher education, presenting its most salient features from a broadly sociocultural perspective. In the next section, I present a brief summary of some of the studies in which reflective practices have been used to sensitise teachers to the importance of an understanding of classroom discourse, where professional development has been enhanced through closer understandings of classroom interaction.

1.3 TEACHER DEVELOPMENT AND CLASSROOM DISCOURSE

This section surveys some of the research which has been conducted within the field of teacher development and classroom discourse, critically reviewing those studies which have set out to train second language teachers to make better use of their verbal behaviour, or enhance awareness of interactional processes. At the end of this section, a table has been added summarising each of these (and other) studies.

A number of calls have been made by researchers in recent years for teachers to discover for themselves what kinds of interaction foster learning and what the role of the teacher is in creating and managing that interaction:

> The challenge set before teachers is to recognize both the obvious in their classrooms and the not so obvious within themselves and their students, to understand how both of these dimensions shape the dynamics of classroom communication, and to equip their second language students with the competencies they need to get the most out of their second language experiences. (Johnson 1995: 169)

For teachers to implement pedagogical intentions effectively … it is important [for them] to develop an understanding of the interactional organisation of the L2 classroom. (Seedhouse 1997: 574)

The challenge for teachers of ESL students [is] to find out more about the types of interaction that occur in their classrooms, and to also reflect on teaching practice and curriculum implementation which have the potential to facilitate second language development in the classroom context. (Glew 1998: 5)

Any endeavour to improve teaching and learning should begin by looking at classroom interaction. Everything which occurs in the classroom requires the use of language. Crucially, in a classroom, it is through language in interaction that we access new knowledge, acquire and develop new skills, identify problems of understanding, deal with 'breakdowns' in the communication, establish and maintain relationships and so on. (Walsh 2011: 122)

Most of the studies on classroom interaction are descriptive rather than pedagogic in nature (Thompson 1997: 99), concerned with developing further understandings of the process of second language acquisition in the formal context. While these studies have certainly increased understanding of the ways in which languages are learnt, they are less accessible to the very people they are intended to influence: language teachers. In the remainder of this section, I present findings from a number of studies conducted over the last twenty years or so and designed to help teachers improve their interactional competence through reflective practices.

1.3.1 Richards (1990)

With the focus on teachers' questioning strategies, Richards (1990) reports the findings of a training 'minicourse' which set out to improve teachers' questioning skills through the use of film, self-evaluation and micro-teaching. The quantitative results, summarised below, showed a marked improvement in questioning strategies:

Questioning technique	Before training (frequency)	After training (frequency)
Thought-provoking questions	37.3%	52.0%
Prompting questions	8.5%	13.9%
Repetition of teacher questions	13.7%	4.7%
Teacher answering own questions	4.6%	0.7%

This study underlines the fact that teachers can be trained to ask more appropriate (indeed, fewer) questions and hints at the positive results in terms of learner involvement that such strategies can bring. (By way of contrast, in an earlier study, which also used a quantitative methodology, researchers found that in a typical 50-minute lesson, on average 200 questions were asked, to which 41 per cent received no reply! See White and Lightbown 1984: 229).

The results summarised by Richards indicate quite clearly a change in the teachers' questioning strategies and the increased potential for learner involvement. Awareness-raising, incorporating reflective practices and using data from teachers' own lessons can have far-reaching effects on what students learn and increase opportunities for meaningful participation. While little mention is made here of learner language and the strategies used to make sense of classroom discourse (but see, for example, Breen 1998; Coyle 1999), suffice it to say that learners, as end-users of teacher input have the most to gain from effective questioning. Other researchers have enjoyed similar success in influencing teachers' ability to ask questions (see below, Thornbury 1996; Thompson 1997).

1.3.2 Johnson (1990)

In a study conducted among Hong Kong secondary school teachers, Johnson set up a fifteen-hour 'Classroom Language' training programme, focusing specifically on developing language awareness in the second language classroom. In addition to raising awareness among teachers about their use of language, this programme trained them in the use of effective strategies for increasing learner involvement. Using a variety of techniques and tasks, including language laboratories, the study enhanced awareness of various aspects of classroom language. Through reflective practices centred on the teacher-participants' lesson transcripts, trainees were made aware of three different aspects of their classroom language (Johnson 1990: 273): the first, physiological, essentially related to their voice quality; the second, interpersonal, was connected to the language associated with class management. The third aspect, pedagogical, was broken down into three modes (operative, interactive, informative) based essentially on functional moves such as soliciting, framing and evaluating which stemmed from previous frameworks for analysing classroom discourse (Sinclair and Coulthard 1975; Sinclair and Brazil 1982).

The relevance of Johnson's study to this book lies in the fact that there was a recognition in the 1990 study that classroom discourse is dynamic and constantly shifting, reflected in the teaching methodology and use of language. In particular, the study instilled in teachers an understanding that language use should vary according to pedagogic goals.

1.3.3 Thornbury (1996)

The focus of Thornbury's study was the degree of communicativeness in classroom interaction, motivated by observations made in earlier studies such as 'in communicative classrooms, interactions may … not be very communicative after all' (Nunan 1987: 144). The lack of *genuine* communication in the contemporary second language classroom, the focus of the Thornbury study, has been criticised more overtly by other researchers such as Legutke and Thomas (1991).

Thornbury's study recognises the value of lesson transcripts in raising awareness among trainees and identifies a number of features of communicative classroom talk:

- Referential questions, which require greater effort and depth of processing on the part of the teacher; one possible reason for language teachers' preference for display questions over referential questions (Thornbury 1996: 282).
- Content feedback, where the focus is on meaning.
- Wait-time. Earlier studies confirmed that slight increases in wait-time result in an increase in the quantity and quality of learner contributions and an increase in the number of learner questions.
- Student-initiated talk. Requests for clarification and confirmation checks point to ownership of the discourse (1996: 282) and suggest that learning, through negotiated meaning, is taking place.

Trainees in the Thornbury study were asked to record, transcribe and analyse one segment of a lesson, identifying those features of their talk which were felt to be more or less communicative, and commenting on them in a written evaluation. As Thornbury notes, the real value of the project came not in the written assignment, but in the increased communicativeness of the trainees' classroom teaching (1996: 283). The conclusions are mixed, with an assertion, on the one hand, that teachers can be sensitised to classroom discourse which is communicative, while, on the other, acknowledging that the process of changing teacher behaviour is neither 'painless nor linear' (1996: 287). The following point is also made concerning the importance of the learner:

> Nor do adjustments to teacher talk have much long-term effect if the teacher is not committed to the belief that student-centredness is more than a matter of providing pair and group-work … the training programme must also address the larger concern of the learner's personal investment in the language learning process. (1996: 287)

1.3.4 Bailey (1996)

Bailey addressed teachers' decision-making and looked at the ways in which teachers' interactive decisions cause them to depart from their lesson plan. Bailey's concern was to get an emic (insider) perspective, using teachers' voices to gain an understanding of how decisions to depart from what was planned were made. Using a stimulated recall methodology, teacher-participants were asked to view extracts of their lesson where they had departed from their lesson-plan and justify the interactional decisions taken. Several reasons for teachers' departures from what was planned were then summarised as five principles of interactive decision-making (Bailey 1996: 27–36). Bailey acknowledges that there may well be other reasons for teachers' 'online' decision-making (1996: 36) and that another group of teachers may employ a different set of interactive principles.

Nonetheless, the principal merit of the study lies in its underlying philosophy: an endeavour to attain an emic perspective on interactional decision-making which draws on the voices and stories of the teachers, retold by the researcher; that is, findings were co-produced by the teachers and the researcher, not by the researcher alone. Given an appropriate context and the interactional space needed (Mann 2001: 58), second language teachers are more than capable of articulating the interactive decisions they make, even when those decisions are unplanned. Good teaching is based on far more than 'planfulness' (Leinhardt and Greeno 1986: 76). As Bailey demonstrates quite clearly, skilled teaching is about the interactive choices which are made online, about the decisions which are taken in the fast flow of the lesson. Perhaps more importantly, good interactive decision-making can be *acquired* by sensitising teachers to the alternatives open to them, using the kinds of reflective practices described by Bailey.

1.3.5 Tsui (1996)

Like Richards (1990), the context for this study is Hong Kong secondary schools. In Tsui (1996), the focus of investigation is learner reticence, building on previous studies addressing this important phenomenon which characterises so much of learner behaviour in some parts of the world (see, for example, Wu 1991). Much learner discourse in larger classes is characterised by single-word responses, whispered replies to teacher prompts, or silence (Tsui 1996: 145). In the same context, learner-initiated clarification requests and learner questions simply never occurred. In an earlier study, again in the Hong Kong secondary classroom context, Tsui (1985) reports that teacher talk accounted for 80 per cent of the total talk time, with silence and frequently repeated teacher questions predominant features of the discourse. Under such conditions, with minimal participation, it is unlikely that much is being learnt at all (Allwright and Bailey 1991); there is no negotiated meaning and hypotheses about the second language are not being tested in the form of learner contributions (Swain 1985, 1995). For the teachers in the 1996 study, getting learners to talk was a major problem with over 70 per cent identifying this as their over-riding concern (Tsui 1996: 146).

Tsui reports findings from a two-year in-service teacher education programme in which teachers were required to make one video or audio recording of a lesson, identify one problem in their classes, devise strategies to overcome the problem, try them out and then evaluate the whole process in a later lesson. The problem of learner reticence manifested itself in a number of ways according to teacher perceptions. These included: a lack of self-confidence or willingness to take risks; a fear of mistakes and derision; a fear (on the part of teachers) of silence; an uneven distribution of turns, with teacher bids going mainly to the brighter learners; incomprehensible input – teachers' contributions were too vague or too difficult to understand. The practitioners in the study reported a number of strategies used to overcome the inter-actional problems they had identified (1996: 160–4):

(a) Lengthening wait-time. Silence was considered to be a waste of time because, as one teacher commented, 'time is too precious'. Earlier studies confirm that teachers do not allow sufficient wait-time owing to a need to cover the syllabus and a fear that silence results in boredom and a loss of pace in the lesson (White and Lightbown

1984: 236). Similar reasons were given by teachers in the 1996 study. However, Tsui also reports that while silence is 'not necessarily a bad thing', excessive wait-time can increase learner anxiety.

(b) Improving questioning strategies. Like other researchers, Tsui notes that one of the strategies identified by the teachers in the study was to improve their questioning strategies by asking more referential questions and fewer display questions. While an increase in referential questions did not necessarily result in longer or better learner responses, allowing planning time to answer those questions did; some teachers commented on the value of getting students to write down their answers before verbalising them.

(c) Accepting a variety of answers. Allowing a variety of responses and emphasising that there was no one 'right' answer was found to be of some value in initiating learner responses, with one teacher allowing learners three choices after each question: answer, ask for help, or ask for more time.

(d) Making use of group work and peer support. Interaction in the 'safety' of a group before open class feedback was found to be effective as a means of getting students to speak out, since it allowed rehearsal in a 'low risk, high gain situation' (1996: 163).

(e) Content feedback. Content feedback was found to be effective since learners knew that their errors would not be corrected.

In conclusion, Tsui suggests that a greater awareness of effective anxiety-reducing strategies is needed if language learning is to be made a more productive and enjoyable experience (1996: 165). Implicit in her remarks is the suggestion that teachers need to be sensitised to strategies which are effective in reducing anxiety, again by reflecting on classroom recordings and having opportunities to discuss them.

1.3.6 Thompson (1997)

Like so many other researchers before him, Thompson considers the importance of questioning in the EFL classroom, once again highlighting the need for language teaching professionals to ask appropriate questions and the complexity attached to good questioning. Here, the context is an initial teacher education programme and the concern is to help trainees categorise question types as a way of helping them identify options. A three-way classification of questions was devised, enabling questions to be analysed according to:

(a) Form. Essentially, this is a grammatical categorisation: whether the questions are closed or open (Hargreaves 1984), or, more traditionally, *yes/no* or *wh-*. The distinction is important since closed questions are easier to answer than open ones (Gower et al. 1995); asking a closed question may facilitate involvement in the form of a short answer, which can then be followed with an open *wh-* questions to extend the learner's contribution (Thompson 1997: 100).

(b) Content. The focus of the question may relate to personal facts, outside facts or opinions. While the value of 'personalising' questions cannot be denied, since it often results in increased learner investment in the discourse, Thompson argues that 'personalisation does not necessarily mean that real communication is taking place' (1997: 101).

(c) Purpose. The distinction here is between questions which are for display and questions which are for communication. The case for referential questions has been stated elsewhere (see, for example, Brock 1986; Tsui 1996). According to Thompson, the distinction between display and referential questions is over-stated (see also van Lier 1988; Seedhouse 1996). The real issue is the extent to which teachers *behave* as if they know the answer to a question; genuine communication can be facilitated when teachers act as if they do not know the answer to a question or deliberately ask questions (about learners' culture or professional background) to which they do not know the answer.

The main value of the framework lies in its potential to make practitioners think about their choice of question in relation to what they are doing in the classroom and, more importantly, about their role in the interaction; a realisation, for example, that student contributions do not always have to be evaluated (Thompson 1997: 105). Arguably, the framework has even greater potential for raising awareness when used in conjunction with teacher-generated data such as audio recordings and/or lesson transcripts as against the reading texts employed in the original study.

1.3.7 Cullen (1998)

In this study, Cullen makes a case for understanding teacher talk, suggesting that there is a need to analyse teachers' use of language from a *qualitative* rather than *quantitative* perspective. 'Good' teacher talk does not necessarily mean 'little' teacher talk; rather effective teacher talk 'facilitates learning and promotes communicative interaction' (Cullen 1998: 179). Citing three reasons for this shift in emphasis – teacher talk is a valuable source of comprehensible input (Krashen 1985); teacher educators have been powerless in eradicating teacher talk; in many parts of the world, high levels of teacher talk are expected – Cullen posits the concept of 'communicative teacher talk' (1998: 180).

Following Thornbury (1996, see above), the researcher suggests that the communicativeness of classroom discourse should be judged in accordance with what constitutes 'communicative' in that context, as opposed to what is communicative in other social contexts. Models of communication which constantly compare the second language classroom with the 'real world' are unrealistic and may be unattainable for many teachers; put simply, the classroom has to be treated as a context in its own right – any attempt to judge the communicativeness of teacher (or learner) talk should be made in relation to what is meant by 'communicative' in that context (1998: 182).

Four features of communicative teacher talk are identified – referential questions, content feedback, speech modifications, negotiation of meaning – in addition to features of non-communicative teacher talk which include excessive use of display questions, form-focused feedback, teacher echo, sequences of IRF discourse chains (1998: 182). Any analysis of the communicative value of teacher talk should take account not only of its ability to foster meaningful communication among learners, but also of the extent to which it coincides with the teacher's pedagogic purpose. For example, the communicativeness of an instruction would be measured in terms of how well that instruction was carried out or the extent to which it permitted negotiation of meaning or clarification by learners.

While the study does not suggest how this framework might be used in sensitising teachers to the communicativeness of their talk, it is not difficult to imagine how reflective practices, using class-based recordings, could be incorporated in an awareness-raising process. Teachers, in evaluating the communicativeness of their talk, would assess the extent to which their use of language coincided with intended learning outcomes.

1.3.8 Walsh (2006)

In this study, Walsh set out to help a small group of university language teachers improve their interactional competence through the use of SETT: self-evaluation of teacher talk and guided reflective practice. Building on the work of other researchers (see, for example, Seedhouse 2004), Walsh identified four classroom micro-contexts which he called *modes*. Each mode has its own distinctive interactional features aligned with specific pedagogic goals. Walsh argues that by using a modes analysis and the accompanying SETT framework, teachers' classroom interactional competence can be significantly improved, resulting in more dialogic, engaged and active learning environments. A full discussion of this work is presented in Chapter 4.

In the remainder of this section, several key strands are highlighted from the studies reviewed above as having particular relevance to this book:

(a) Sensitising teachers to a greater understanding of classroom discourse stems, in the first instance, from a concern to enhance learning. While the term 'teacher talk' immediately conjures up images of teacher-centredness, most of the studies reviewed here are motivated by a concern for the learners. Johnson (1990) considers the use of appropriate questioning strategies to increase learner involvement; Bailey (1996) was concerned to help teachers understand why they made interactive decisions – decisions which were exclusively guided by the learners; Tsui's study (1996) was motivated by learner reticence, while Harrison (1996) considered modifications to learners' verbal behaviour, instigated by modified teacher language in a process of curriculum renewal. Learners are central and instrumental to the process of enhancing teachers' understanding of classroom interaction, and, ultimately, have the most to gain.

(b) Reflective practices are more easily accomplished when teachers analyse their own data. In several of the studies, teachers' awareness was raised primarily by getting them to record, transcribe and analyse their lessons using an instrument to facilitate evaluation (Johnson 1990; Thornbury 1996; Tsui 1996; Bailey 1996; Cadorath and Harris 1998). I would suggest that reflective practices are far more likely to succeed if practitioners have a clear focus, an instrument, and use data from their own classes on which to reflect. Simply asking teachers to 'reflect' is insufficient and may lead, at best, to fuzzy understandings and uncertain changes to practice.

(c) An emic (insider) perspective, relying on teachers' voices, actions and stories is more conducive to gaining a true understanding of interactional processes in the L2 classroom than the imposed perspective of the researcher. An insider perspective is also easier to obtain when teacher-participants are encouraged to verbalise their experiences in a co-constructed interview. Bailey, for example, used stimulated recall to initiate dialogue; Tsui used post-teaching interviews, while Thornbury preferred a form of written self-evaluation. Each procedure has its own merits and can be adapted according to local conditions.

(d) The complexities of classroom interaction in the L2 context can be best under-stood when data are collected using a variety of instruments: a multi-mode method. Apart from enhancing reliability and validity, multi-mode methods of data collection ensure that 'all the angles are covered', that the setting is viewed from more than one position. Harrison, for example, uses lesson observations and transcripts, reports and evaluative comments from teachers to assess changes in teachers' verbal behaviour; Tsui makes use of video recordings, lesson transcripts, self-evaluations and written reports. Teacher-participants also respond differently to stimuli for reflection (see Harrison 1996 above), another reason for using multiple data sources.

(e) In several of the studies, there is considerable overlap in the interactional features which were 'targeted'. For example, Tsui, Thornbury, Cullen, Thompson and Cadorath and Harris all recognise the importance of specific questioning strategies and the need to allow increased wait-time to promote learner involvement. Tsui, Thornbury and Cullen mention the value of content feedback and negotiated mean-ing. Perhaps not surprisingly, the need for teachers to address questioning strategies still receives the greatest amount of attention, while there appears to be a growing realisation that the L2 classroom has to be treated as a context in its own right: any attempt to understand L2 classroom communication must recognise the relationship which prevails between pedagogic goals and language use.

What I hope is now apparent is the fact that teachers' professional development can, and indeed, should, be aided by making classroom discourse the main focus of attention. An understanding of the role of interaction in learning, of the importance of appropriate language use, of the need to develop specific interactional strategies, and of the value of acquiring classroom interactional competence lie at the very heart of second language teacher professional development. In the remainder of this book, we will explore how this process of teacher development through classroom discourse can be brought about.

Table 1.1   Summary of main teacher development and classroom discourse studies (1990–2006)

Year	Author	Methodology	Main findings
1990	Richards	Intervention and training.	With training, teachers' questioning strategies improved.
1990	Johnson	Various RP methods.	Teachers can be taught to tailor language use to pedagogic goals.
1996	Thornbury	Teachers analysed their own classroom data.	Teachers can be trained to use more 'communicative' language while teaching.
1996	Bailey	Transcripts and interviews with teachers.	Teachers have specific reasons for their 'online decision-making' which may lead them to deviate from their plan.
1996	Tsui	Teacher analysis of their own classroom audio and video recordings.	Teachers can help students overcome reticence by using a range of communication strategies.
1997	Thompson	A three-way classification of questioning strategies used to develop awareness.	Teachers can be trained to ask more effective questions which promote more active learning.
1998	Cullen	*Communicative teacher talk framework* used for awareness-raising.	Identified four features of communicative teacher talk which promote dialogue and engagement.
2006	Walsh	*SETT: self evaluation of teacher talk* framework used to promote teacher awareness.	Teachers can be trained to make better use of language in relation to their specific pedagogic goals.

1.4 CHALLENGES FOR TEACHERS AND LEARNERS

Based on the discussion so far, what challenges might lie ahead for teachers and learners in terms of classroom discourse and language teaching? In this necessarily brief discussion, I posit a number of potential issues and return to these in later chapters.

One of the biggest challenges, based on the research to date, is how to make teachers more aware of the importance of an understanding of classroom interaction. Most teacher education programmes, either pre- or in-service, pay very little attention to classroom interaction. Typically, they provide subject-based preparation and training in classroom methodology; a model comprising two strands which is used all over the world. I would like to see a 'third strand' on teacher education programmes which deals specifically with interaction in the classroom. The aim would be to sensitise language teachers to the centrality of interaction to teaching and learning and provide them with the means of acquiring closer understandings of their local contexts. I suggest that classroom processes will only improve once teachers have the means of understanding local context and are able to improve it. Classroom interaction lies at the heart of this.

Related to this challenge is a desire to see teachers gain 'classroom interactional competence' (CIC). Although this is given a fuller treatment in Chapter 3, it is worth introducing it briefly here. When we analyse classroom transcripts or observe teaching, it is immediately obvious that levels of interactional competence vary hugely from one context and from one teacher to another. Some teachers, at some points in time, are very adept at managing interaction in such a way that learning and learning opportunities are maximised. For example, they may provide opportunities for learners to hold the floor for extended periods, or use interactional strategies to help learners express themselves better. At other stages in a lesson, teachers may, unknowingly, use interactional strategies which 'get in the way' and which impede opportunities for learning (Walsh 2002).

I define CIC as 'teachers' and learners' ability to use interaction as a tool for mediating and assisting learning' (Walsh 2011: 132). The assumption is that by first understanding and then extending CIC, there will be greater opportunities for learning: enhanced CIC results in more learning-oriented interactions. Teachers demonstrate CIC in a number of ways. For example, ensuring that language use and pedagogic goals are aligned is an important characteristic of CIC. Other features include the use of extended wait-time: allowing a reasonable time to elapse after asking a question and not interrupting students all the time; extending learner responses by careful management of the interaction and paraphrasing a learner's utterance, for example. Similarly, teachers need to be able to help learners as and when needed by scaffolding a contribution, offering a key piece of vocabulary or introducing a new phrase as and when needed, for example. Achieving CIC will only happen if teachers are able to understand interactional processes and make changes to the ways in which they manage classroom interaction.

Other challenges facing teachers in the future is the need to gain a fuller understanding of the relationship between classroom methodologies and classroom interaction. This will be dealt with more fully in Chapter 2, but suffice it to say here that a closer understanding of how interactional features manifest themselves in, for example, task-based learning, can only be of benefit to teachers and learners alike. How does task-type affect interaction and what is the consequence for learning? How might more effective management of classroom interaction result in a more engaged, more dialogic type of learning? And what do we know of the importance of interaction during feedback following a task? This, according to many researchers, is the most important part of the task-based cycle and the one most likely to lead to learning. There is much work to do in this area.

Similarly, a further challenge is how to integrate technology in a way which promotes, rather than impedes, classroom interaction. While advances in educational technology are occurring at an alarming rate, the speed at which they are being integrated successfully into effective language teaching is taking place at a much slower pace. There is, then, a need for research which looks at the impact of technology on interaction, and on the consequences of learning processes which are mediated not only by language, but also by technology (for example, CMC: computer mediated communication).

From a learner's perspective, a number of challenges lie ahead. Perhaps the biggest and most difficult one is the need to promote more equal interactions between teachers and learners. When we consider the ways in which learners are socialised into certain types of classroom behaviour, this is a huge challenge. In most content-based subjects, learners answer questions, respond to cues, follow the teacher's initiative, avoid interrupting and so on. And yet, in a language classroom, a very different set of interactional traits is needed if learners are to play a more equal part in the discourse. Here, we need learners to both ask and answer questions, to interrupt where appropriate, to take the initiative, seize the floor, hold a turn and so on. By following learnt behaviours which are the product of many years of being socialised into classroom rituals and practices, we may be facilitating the kind of 'smooth' discourse profile which prevails at the moment. But are we helping to create interactions which result in learning? I suggest that we need to encourage interactions which have a more 'jagged' profile in which learners play a more central role in co-constructing meanings and in ensuring that there are opportunities for negotiation, clarification and the like. A jagged classroom interaction profile has more of the features which would be found in naturally occurring interactions such as everyday conversation, business encounters and the like. While not denying that the language classroom is a social context in its own right, many of its features are determined by the fact that control of the communication lies with the teacher. In other contexts, roles are much more equal, resulting in different interactional features. Turns are longer, for example, and there are more frequent topic changes. Overlaps and interruptions are more common, as are pauses. I am suggesting that it is in this kind of interaction that learners have the opportunity to acquire the kinds of linguistic and interactional resources which will help them develop as learners. Teachers, while still playing a more central role, would need a far more sophisticated understanding of classroom discourse in order to be able to manage the interaction.

In the final section of this chapter, I present an overview of the rest of the book.

1.5 OVERVIEW OF THE BOOK

Chapter 2 considers what we can learn about teaching by looking at classroom discourse. The chapter begins with an overview of discourse and an evaluation of its importance to both an understanding of language learning and a means of promoting development. The discussion then turns to a more detailed examination of classroom discourse by addressing questions such as: What are the main features of classroom discourse in a second language classroom? How can these features be studied? What are the relative merits and disadvantages of the various approaches used for studying classroom discourse such as discourse analysis, interaction analysis, conversation analysis? More importantly, what does an understanding of these features tell us about learning and teaching and how can we use data from our own teaching to improve our professional practice?

Chapter 3 evaluates how notions of learning through interaction can be extended by looking at the ways in which interactants display varying degrees of classroom interactional competence (CIC). The assumption is that by first understanding and then extending CIC, there will be greater opportunities for learning: enhanced CIC results in more learning-oriented interactions, greater engagement among learners and more active learning environments.

In Chapter 4, a framework is presented for helping teachers gain a closer understanding of their own classroom discourse: the SETT (self-evaluation of teacher talk) framework, comprising four classroom micro-contexts (called *modes*) and fourteen interactional features (called *interactures*) (see Walsh 2006). Spoken classroom language is portrayed as a series of complex and inter-related micro-contexts (modes), where meanings are co-constructed by teachers and learners and where learning occurs through the ensuing talk of teachers and learners. The same framework is scrutinised more closely in Chapter 5 which looks at how SETT might be applied across a range of contexts, including both teaching and teacher education, as a means of promoting awareness and helping teachers to develop CIC.

In Chapter 5, the discussion turns to a consideration of how teachers might gain closer understandings of their use of language and management of interaction as a means of promoting a more engaged, dynamic classroom atmosphere. A range of 'tools' is presented, designed to help teachers gain closer understandings of interactional processes while avoiding the need for wholesale transcription. More established approaches to professional development (such as critical reflective practice, exploratory practice) are critiqued and compared.

Chapter 6 offers a critique of reflective practice, proposing that the construct needs to be revisited and revitalised if it is to succeed. In this chapter, a call is made for an approach to RP which is more collaborative, more dialogic, data-led and reflexive in order to replace the current position in which RP is largely viewed as an institutional requirement which is undertaken in a written format.

In the final chapter of the book, Chapter 7, I consider how teachers can use an enhanced understanding of interaction in their teaching and how we can all become researchers of our own practice. The main argument in this chapter is that teachers can continue to grow and improve their practice by constantly paying close attention to the interactions taking place while teaching. By gaining close understandings of interactional processes, I suggest that all teachers can learn to make better 'online' decisions (decisions made while teaching) and promote more active and engaged classrooms. In this way, we can all become researchers of our practice in the true sense, with the ultimate goal of improving the learning experience of our students.

Chapter 2

Classroom discourse: an overview

This chapter presents an overview of the key features of second language classroom interaction. It describes and characterises the most common classroom practices and their discourse features, using extracts from English language lessons. The aim is to offer a sketch of classroom discourse, as opposed to a detailed description, since many of the themes and issues raised here will be dealt with in more detail in the rest of the book. The chapter is divided into four sections. In the first section, I offer an overview of discourse analysis, aimed primarily at readers who have little or no knowledge of this field, and focused on the analysis of spoken discourse from the perspectives of pragmatics and conversation analysis. In the next section, the discussion looks at the specific features of classroom discourse: its structure and inherent interactional properties. This is followed by a critique of the single, most common types of exchange structure found in all classrooms: IRF, a three-part exchange, comprising teacher Initiation, learner Response and teacher Feedback. In the final section of this chapter, we consider the various approaches which can be used to study classroom discourse, including discourse analysis, interaction analysis and conversation analysis.

2.1 DISCOURSE AND DISCOURSE ANALYSIS

Discourse means written or spoken texts which have been produced in a particular context or for a specific purpose. Discourse analysis is the study of spoken or written texts as a means of understanding their internal and external structure or logic (cf. McCarthy 1992; Gee 2005). For example, when studying spoken texts, we might be interested in the ways in which interlocutors co-construct meanings or establish mutual understandings. Discourse analysis is the umbrella term for analysing longer stretches of spoken or written language in context. Here, we are only concerned with spoken texts, which can be analysed using a range of discourse analytic approaches including conversation analysis, pragmatics, critical discourse analysis and so on.

In this necessarily brief introduction, I will focus only on pragmatics and conversation analysis since they have the most direct relevance to the main academic enterprise of this book.

2.1.1 Pragmatics

> **TASK 2.1**
> In each of the situations below, there is a communication problem. What caused the problem and how could it have been avoided?

A

A British teacher working in China told a group of students that they 'might like to do' an exercise in the course-book for homework. The next day, the students were surprised and embarrassed to find that the teacher expected them to have done the homework.

(From Spencer-Oatey and Žegarac 2002: 87)

B

Father of a six year old on the phone to 'Grandma':

Father: Would you like to say hello to Grandma now?
Child: No thank you.

C

A commuter is at a Metro station with a $20 bill, and no fare card. She approaches a Metro employee.

Commuter: Do you know where I can get change for $20?
Employee: You'll have to go into a store or something.
Commuter: Well there's really nothing nearby.
            What should I do?
Employee: What you should do is check your money before you leave home and
            Make sure you have the right change.

(B and C from Schiffrin 1994)

It is immediately obvious from each of these scenarios that misunderstandings occur because a speakers' intended meaning has been misconstrued by their audience. Put differently, the locutionary force of their utterances (literal meaning) was in some way different to the illocutionary force (intended meaning). Effective communication, then, depends on the extent to which interactants infer meaning correctly, which, in turn, depends on our ability to frame an utterance in the most appropriate way for our listeners. As Grundy puts it:

> Communication is not merely a matter of a speaker encoding a thought in language and sending it as spoken message through space, or as a written message on paper, to a receiver who decodes it. This is clearly insufficient – the receiver must not only decode what is received but also draw an inference as to what is conveyed beyond what is stated. (2000: 7)

Pragmatics, then, is the study of meaning in context. Rather than simply looking at the words themselves, pragmatics considers all the contextual features of an utterance in a bid to make sense of what was *meant*, rather than what was *said*. One way of thinking about this is to consider the ways in which we read or listen 'between the lines' to infer meaning; the words themselves are, in one sense, less important than the meaning which lies behind them. According to Atkinson et al., pragmatics is 'the distinction between what a speaker's words (literally) mean and what the speaker might mean by his words' (1988: 217). Consider, for example, the simple utterance *the window's open*. How might the actual meaning of this utterance change according to who said it, where and so on? (see Cook 1989).

Thomas (1995) defines pragmatics as *meaning in interaction*. In this sense, meaning is regarded as a dynamic variable which entails negotiation of meaning between speaker and listeners according to the particular context in which it is said and the meaning potential of that utterance. This view of pragmatics has particular relevance to the study of classroom discourse, where any single utterance might be interpreted in any number of ways according to context.

Pragmatics, then, is concerned to address questions such as:

- How do people communicate more than what the words or phrases of their utterances might mean by themselves, and how do people make these interpretations?
- Why do people choose to say and/or interpret something in one way rather than another?
- How do people's perceptions of contextual factors (for example, who the interlocutors are, what their relationship is, and what circumstances they are communicating in) influence the process of producing and interpreting language?

Essentially, pragmatics is concerned to develop an understanding of how interactants make sense of their intended meanings in context, as opposed to operating at the decontextualised level of literal meanings of 'the words on a page'. Participants in a dialogue achieve mutual understanding, from a pragmatics perspective, by drawing upon a range of resources, including the assignment of reference in context, the assignment of sense in context, the interpretation of illocutionary force and the interpretation of implicated meaning. For communication to proceed smoothly, it is apparent that interactants make use of a whole host of contextual features, which they deploy and interpret in a highly skilled and sophisticated way. Acquiring pragmatic competence (see Hymes 1972, 1996) is arguably one of the most difficult things to do in any second language, and, of course, the one which creates the most problems when it is not acquired to any adequate standard.

2.1.2 Conversation analysis

The origins of conversation analysis (CA) lie in sociology, not linguistics or applied linguistics. The original interest arose out of a perceived need to study ordinary conversation as social action; CA's underlying philosophy is that social contexts are not static but are constantly being formed by participants through their use of language and the ways in which turn-taking, openings and closures, sequencing of acts and so on are locally managed (Sacks, Schegloff and Jefferson 1974). Interaction is examined in relation to meaning and context; the way in which actions are sequenced is central to the process. In the words of Heritage:

> In fact, CA embodies a theory which argues that sequences of actions are a major part of what we mean by context, that the meaning of an action is heavily shaped by the sequence of previous actions from which it emerges, and that social context is a dynamically created thing that is expressed in and through the sequential organisation of interaction. (1997: 162)

According to this view, interaction is *context-shaped* and *context-renewing*; that is, one contribution, or 'turn-at-talk' is dependent on a previous one, and subsequent contributions create a new context for later actions. Context is 'both a project and a product of the participants' actions' (Heritage 1997: 163). Although the original focus of CA was naturally occurring conversation, it is perhaps in specific institutional settings, where the goals and actions of participants are clearly determined, that the value of CA approaches can be most vividly realised. The discussion turns briefly to an institutional discourse perspective before looking specifically at CA in the L2 classroom.

An institutional discourse CA methodology takes as its starting point the centrality of talk to many work tasks: quite simply, the majority of work-related tasks are completed through what is essentially conversation, or 'talk-in-interaction' (Drew and Heritage 1992: 3); many interactions (for example, doctor-patient interviews, court-room examinations of a witness, classrooms) are completed through the exchange of talk between specialist and non-specialists: 'Talk-in-interaction is the principal means through which lay persons pursue various practical goals and the central medium through which the daily lives of many professionals and organizational representatives are conducted' (Drew and Heritage 1992: 3).

The purpose of a CA methodology in an institutional setting is to account for the ways in which context is created for and by the participants in relation to the goal-oriented activity in which they are engaged (Heritage 1997: 163). All institutions have an over-riding goal or purpose which constrains both the actions and interactional contributions of the participants according to the business in hand, giving each institution a unique interactional 'fingerprint' (Heritage and Greatbatch 1991: 95–6). Thus, the interactional patterning (or 'fingerprint') which is typical of, for example, a travel agent will be different from that of a classroom and different again from that of a doctor's surgery. In each context, there are well-defined roles and expectations which, to some extent, determine what is said.

By examining specific features in the institutional interaction, an understanding can be gained of the ways in which context is both constructed and sustained; features which can be usefully examined include turn-taking organisation, turn design, sequence organisation, lexical choice and asymmetry of roles (Heritage 1997). The second language classroom is, of course, a clear example of an institutional setting with asymmetrical roles, goal-oriented activities and a context which is constantly being created for and by participants through the classroom interaction. While the discourse of L2 classrooms does not and should not be interpreted as having any resemblance to conversation, there are nonetheless good reasons for using a CA methodology:

> The point is not that classroom talk 'should' resemble conversation, since most of the time for practical purposes it cannot, but that institutionalised talk ... shows a heightened use of procedures which have their 'base' in ordinary conversation and are more clearly understood through comparison with it. (Edwards and Westgate 1994: 116)

The relevance of a CA approach to the L2 classroom context is not difficult to perceive. CA attempts to account for the practices at work which enable participants in a conversation to make sense of the interaction and contribute to it. There are clear parallels: classroom talk is made up of many participants; it involves turn-taking, -ceding, -holding and -gaining; there have to be smooth transitions and clearly defined expectations if meanings are to be made explicit. Possibly the most significant role of CA is to *interpret* from the data rather than *impose* pre-determined categories.

One of the biggest influences on CA-led classroom-based research was the call of Firth and Wagner (1997) for greater sensitivity towards contextual and interactional aspects of language use by focusing more on the participants in SLA research and less on cognitive processes. Since the late 1990s, these studies have highlighted the ways in which learning and interactional competence can be approached and described through a micro-analytic mode of inquiry (see, for example, Hellermann 2008; Markee 2008; Pekarek-Doehler 2010). From this body of research has emerged the field now known as CA-SLA or CA-for-SLA: Conversation Analysis for Second Language Acquisition. By focusing on micro-details of video- or audio-recorded interaction, CA-for-SLA aims to document micro-moments of learning and understanding by drawing upon participants' own understanding of the ongoing interaction, from an emic perspective. This perspective is revealed through a detailed analysis of vocal (words and grammar, suprasegmentals, pace of talk, etc.) and non-vocal (silence, body language, embodiment of surrounding artefacts, etc.) resources within the sequential development of talk. CA-for-SLA studies have succeeded in demonstrating 'good' examples of 'interactional competence' and/or understanding of certain information by students by using interactionally and pedagogically fruitful instances of talk; for instance through the use of repair sequences (e.g., Hellermann 2008).

To summarise this necessarily brief overview of the use of CA for the study of classroom discourse, we can make a number of claims concerning its appropriateness. Firstly, under CA, there is no preconceived set of descriptive categories at the outset. The aim of CA is to account for the structural organisation of the interaction as determined by the participants. That is, there should be no attempt to 'fit' the data to preconceived categories; evidence that such categories exist and are utilised by the participants must be demonstrated by reference to and examples from the data. Thus, the approach is strictly empirical. Secondly, there is a recognition that the context is not static and fixed, but dynamic and variable. A dynamic perspective on context allows for variability; contexts are not fixed entities which operate across a lesson, but dynamic and changing processes which vary from one stage of a lesson to another (Cullen 1998). A CA methodology is better equipped to take variations in linguistic and pedagogic purpose into account since one contribution is dependent on another. Third, the approach recognises that all spoken interactions are goal-oriented. Under institutional discourse, the behaviour and discourse of the participants are goal-oriented in that they are striving towards some overall objective related to the institution. In a language classroom, for example, the discourse is influenced by the fact that all participants are focusing on some pre-determined aim: learning a second language. Different participants, depending on their own agenda may have different individual objectives; nonetheless, the discourse which is jointly constructed is dependent on both the goals and the related expectations of the participants. Finally, CA offers a multi-layered perspective on classroom discourse. Because no one utterance is categorised in isolation and because contributions are examined in sequence, a CA methodology is much better equipped to interpret and account for the multi-layered structure of classroom interaction.

2.2 FEATURES OF CLASSROOM DISCOURSE

Turning now to a discussion of the principal features of classroom discourse, we quickly realise that classroom communication is both highly complex and central to all classroom activity. In the rapid flow of classroom interaction, it is difficult to comprehend what is happening. Not only does the interaction happen very fast and involve many people, it has multiple foci; the language being used may be performing several functions at the same time: seeking information, checking learning, offering advice and so on.

The position adopted throughout this book is that any attempt to improve teaching and learning, any move towards professional development, should begin by looking at the interactions which take place in the classroom. Everything which occurs in the classroom requires the use of language, and interaction underpins every action, every activity and all classroom practices. Crucially, in a classroom, it is through interaction that we access new knowledge, acquire and develop new skills, identify problems of understanding, deal with 'breakdowns' in the communication, establish and maintain relationships and so on. Language, quite simply, lies at the heart of everything. This situation is further complicated when we consider that in a language classroom, the language being used is not only the means of acquiring new knowledge, it is also the *goal* of study: 'the vehicle and object of study' (Long 1983: 37). Another layer of complexity is added in a multilingual classroom setting, where multiple interactions take place between people from a range of linguistic and cultural backgrounds – all performed in a second language.

Yet despite its obvious importance, until recently little time had been given to helping teachers *understand* classroom interaction. While researchers have gone to great lengths to describe the interactional processes of the language classroom, few have used this knowledge to help teachers improve their practices. Most teacher education programmes devote a considerable amount of time to teaching methods and to subject knowledge. Few, I suggest, devote nearly enough time to developing understandings of interactional processes and the relationship between the ways in which language is used to establish, develop and promote understandings. Teachers and learners, arguably, need to acquire what I call 'classroom interactional competence' (CIC, see Walsh 2006, 2011) if they are to work effectively together. That is, teachers and learners must make use of a range of appropriate interactional and linguistic resources in order to promote active, engaged learning. Classroom interactional competence is discussed in full in Chapter 3.

In the remainder of this section, I offer an overview of the most important features of second language classroom discourse. Six features of classroom discourse have been selected, largely because they typify much of the interaction which takes place in classrooms and are prevalent in all parts of the world:

1. Teachers' control of the interaction

2. Speech modification

3. Elicitation

4. Repair

5. Student-student interaction

6. Computer mediated communication (CMC)

2.2.1 Teachers' control of the interaction

As in any institutional discourse setting, the roles of participants are not equal, they are asymmetrical. This is true of all classrooms: primary, secondary, tertiary, monolingual, multilingual, with adult, teenage or very young learners. It is also true of many other contexts, where there are differences of power, authority and knowledge: doctor/patient, solicitor/client, shop assistant/customer and so on. In each of these settings, including classrooms, one party is in a position of power or authority; that person has control of the patterns of communication which occur and is able to direct and manage the interaction. In language classrooms, teachers control patterns of communication by managing both the topic of conversation and turn-taking, while students typically take their cues from the teacher through whom they direct most of their responses. Even in the most decentralised and learner-centred classroom, teachers decide who speaks, when, to whom and for how long. Teachers are able to interrupt when they like, take the floor, hand over a turn, direct the discussion, switch topics. As Breen puts it, it is the teacher who 'orchestrates the interaction' (1998: 119).

While there has, in the past twenty years or so, been a move towards student-centred teaching, learners still do not enjoy the same level of control of the patterns of communication, although there will certainly be times when the roles of teacher and learners are more equal, allowing more even turn-taking and greater participation by learners. For much of the time, learners respond to the cues given by teachers: in the form of a spoken response, an action (such as opening a book, changing seats), or a change of focus (from a powerpoint slide to course-book, for example, or from listening to the teacher to talking to a classmate).

If we look now at some classroom data, we can see quite clearly how teachers control the interaction. Consider extract 2.1 below in which a group of multilingual, intermediate adult learners are discussing issues about law and order in their respective countries (a full account of the transcription conventions used appears in the appendix):

Extract 2.1

1	T:	OK Erica could you explain something about law and order in Japan what
2		happens if you commit a crime?
3	L1:	almost same as Britain policeman come to take somebody to police station
4	T:	yes
5	L1:	and prisoner questioned and if he is ((5))=
6	T:	=yes what's the verb Eric Erica … if she or he yes commits a crime they go
7		to ↑
8	L1:	they go to court yes but if they he they didn't do that they can go home
9	T:	they can go home (…) very good indeed right what happens in Brazil

In line 1, we see how the teacher uses an 'individual nomination' (Mehan 1979) to bring Erica into the discussion. Her question, 'what happens if you commit a crime', both establishes the topic and provides a cue for Erica, who must now provide the second-pair part to the question, a response, which she does in line 3. In line 5, we can see that the learner is experiencing some difficulty and the teacher interrupts in line 6, indicated by = (a latched turn, where one turn follows another without any pausing). Again, in line 6, the teacher is controlling the interaction, seeking clarification and correcting an error ('what's the verb'?). Not only does the teacher control the topic, she steers Erica towards an answer by using a designedly incomplete utterance (Koshik 2002) in lines 6 and 7, 'they go to' (said with a rising intonation). The interactional work performed by the teacher in lines 6 and 7 results in an extended learner turn in line 8, where Erica actually provides more information than that required by the question. Finally, in line 9, the teacher brings L1's contribution to an end 'they can go home', ending L1's participating and inviting another student to make a contribution with the question 'what happens in Brazil?'

Breen's (1998) powerful metaphor of the teacher orchestrating the interaction is in evidence throughout this extract. Arguably, a teacher's ability to 'orchestrate the interaction' in this way not only determines who may participate and when, it influences opportunities for learning. It is also apparent when we look at extract 2.1 that teachers have control over the amount of 'space' learners have in the interaction. For every contribution made by the student, the teacher typically makes two: asking a question (in lines 1 and 6) and giving feedback (in lines 4 and 9). The consequence of this is that teachers clearly talk more and occupy more of the interactional space of the class-room. Learners' opportunities to contribute are largely controlled by the teacher. This three-part discourse structure, comprising a teacher question, learner response and teacher feedback is another feature of classroom discourse which exemplifies the ways in which teachers control the interaction. We'll look at this in some detail below.

2.2.2 Speech modification

One of the defining characteristics of all classroom discourse is teachers' modification of their spoken language. Teachers' use of a more restricted code is, in many respects, similar to the spoken language of parents talking to young children: it is typically slower, louder, more deliberate, and makes greater use of pausing and emphasis. Teachers also make a great deal of use of gestures and facial expressions to help convey meaning. The modification strategies used by teachers are not accidental; they are conscious and deliberate and occur for a number of reasons. The first, and obvious, one is that learners must understand what a teacher is saying if they are going to learn. It is highly unlikely that learners will progress if they do not understand their teacher. A second reason is that, for much of the time, teachers model language for their students. That is, they use appropriate pronunciation, intonation, sentence and word stress and so on, in order to give learners an opportunity to hear the sounds of the target language. In many cases and in many parts of the world, a teacher's articulation of a second language may be the only exposure to the language that learners actually receive. It is important, therefore, that the L2 is modelled correctly and appropriately. A third reason for speech modification is the fact that there is so much happening at any one moment in a classroom that teachers need to ensure that the class is follow-ing, that everyone understands and that learners don't 'get lost' in the rapid flow of the discourse. In his 1998 paper, Michael Breen talks about the need for learners to 'navigate' the discourse and the fact that many learners do actually get lost from time to time. It is the teacher's responsibility to ensure that this does not happen by making frequent use of repetition, by 'echoing' an individual learner's contribution for the benefit of the whole class, by seeking clarification and so on.

An understanding of the ways in which second language teachers modify their speech to learners is clearly important to gaining greater insights into the interactional organisation of the second language classroom and to helping teachers make better use of the strategies open to them. What strategies do teachers use to modify their speech? We can look at modified speech in two ways. On the one hand, teachers employ a different range of linguistic resources to facilitate comprehension and assist the learning process. There are several features of spoken classroom language which teachers normally modify in some way. Perhaps the most obvious one is the use of simplified vocabulary and the absence of more idiomatic or regional variations. Grammar too is frequently simplified through the use of simpler and shorter utterances, the use of a more limited range of tenses and fewer modal verbs.

Pronunciation is also often clearer, with slower articulations and wider use of standard forms. Of course, teachers may ask themselves if they are losing something of their identity by making all these changes. In my experience, this does not happen to any great extent, although teachers do employ their own particular 'classroom idiolect' (Walsh 2001): an individual way of talking which is normally based on their personal conversational style. As we all know, there are features in any speaker's idiolect which may help us understand, and there are certainly other features which possibly 'get in the way' and cause mis-communication.

On another level, teachers modify their interactional resources to assist comprehension and help learners 'navigate the discourse'. Most notable is the use of transition markers to signal the beginnings and endings of various activities or stages in a lesson. Discourse markers like *right, ok, now, so, alright* perform a very important function in signalling changes in the interaction or organisation of learning. They function like punctuation marks on a printed page: consider how difficult it would be to read a newspaper without punctuation. The same applies in a classroom if teachers fail to make appropriate use of transition markers. This important category of discourse markers enables teachers to guide learners through the discourse, hold their attention, announce a change in activity, signal the beginning or end of a lesson stage. Crucially, they help a class 'stay together' and work in harmony.

In addition to the more obvious ways in which teachers modify their speech discussed above, there are other more subtle strategies which teachers use in order to clarify, check or confirm meanings. These include confirmation checks, whereby teachers make sure they understand learners; comprehension checks, ensuring that learners understand the teacher; repetition; clarification requests, asking students for clarification; reformulation, rephrasing a learner's utterance; turn completion, finishing a learner's contribution; backtracking, returning to an earlier part of a dialogue. These strategies highlight the 'jointness' of classroom interaction: teachers and learners work together to co-construct meanings and ensure that the discourse progresses in a smooth manner. This joint enterprise is fundamental to classroom interactional competence; another key element of CIC is teachers' ability to 'shape' learner contributions, a process which requires great skill and mental agility. Shaping entails paraphrasing, reformulating, clarifying and confirming, getting learners to provide more extensive responses, all of which are central to language development and greatly facilitate the learning process.

To better understand this process of what I am calling 'shaping' consider extract 2.2 below. The teacher is working with a group of upper intermediate adult learners and the focus is academic writing. By seeking clarification and by negotiating meaning, the teacher helps the learners to express themselves more fully and more clearly.

Extract 2.2
1 T: =yes so tell me again what you mean by that?=
2 L: =the first is the introduction the second eh in this case we have the ((3))
3   who you are to eh introduce yourself a few words about yourself and where

4   you live and what I do [and]
5   T: [so]…yes?=
6   L: =and then it's the problem what happened …
7   T: yes=
8   L: =and you need to explain it and why you are writing because probably
9   you did something like you gave the information to the police but it didn't
10   happen …
11 T: so can I ask you why did you write it in your head as you said?=
12 L: =I don't know it's like a rule=
13 T: =right so it's like a rule what do you mean? …

Note how learner turns are frequently longer and more complex that those of the teacher. In the extract, this teacher works pretty hard to adopt a more facilitative role, seeking clarification (1, 11, 13) and eliciting from the learner descriptions of their writing strategies. Clarification requests are extremely valuable in promoting opportunities for learning since they 'compel' learners to reformulate their contribution, by rephrasing or paraphrasing. There is clear evidence in this extract that the teacher's unwillingness to accept the learner's first contribution (in 5, 7) promotes a longer and higher quality contribution in 8. Note too how the teacher shows confirmation and understanding (in 7, 13) through the backchannels 'yes' and 'right'. Backchannels are very important in all human interaction since they tell the speaker that the listener has understood and is following what is being said. They 'oil the wheels' of the interaction and ensure that communication occurs (McCarthy 2003).

We have seen, then, that modified speech is a key element of classroom interaction and one which can have profound effects on the quantity and quality of the learning which takes place. Effective speech modification ensures that learners feel safe and included and gives them the confidence to participate in the interaction. It also minimises breakdowns and misunderstandings and creates a sense of purposeful dialogue in which a group of learners is engaged in a collective activity.

2.2.3 Elicitation techniques

Elicitation techniques are the strategies used by (normally) teachers to get learners to respond. Typically, elicitation entails asking questions. Classroom discourse is dominated by question and answer routines, with teachers asking most of the questions, while learners ask correspondingly fewer questions. It is by asking questions that teachers are able to control the discourse and get feedback on what students know or understand; questions like these, where teachers already know the answer (for example, 'what's the past tense of *go*?') are called display questions since they require learners to display what they know. Classrooms are a unique social context since, for much of the time, answers to questions are already known. Asking a question to which you know the answer is the norm in a classroom; in any other context, it would be perceived as being a rather unusual or even odd behaviour.

Display questions serve a range of functions, including:

- Eliciting a response
- Checking understanding
- Guiding learners towards a particular response
- Promoting involvement
- Concept checking

Essentially, the defining characteristic of display questions is to check or evaluate: understanding, concepts, learning, previous learning and so on. Responses tend to be short, simple, restricted, often comprising one or two words. Rather than opening up space for learning, they tend to close it down and result in a rather stereotypical, almost mechanical type of interaction which is often exemplified in IRF sequences (see below).

Apart from display questions, teachers also ask genuine, more open-ended questions, designed to promote discussion and debate, engage learners and produce longer, more complex responses. These so-called referential questions may result in more 'natural' responses by learners, are often longer and more complicated, and may result in a more conversational type of interaction. Referential questions often begin with a *wh-* question such as *who, why, what*, etc. From a teaching and learning perspective, the distinction between display and referential is less important than the relationship between a teacher's pedagogic goal and choice of question. If the aim is to quickly check understanding or establish what learners already know, display questions are perfectly adequate. If, on the other hand, the aim is to promote discussion or help learners improve oral fluency, then referential questions are more appropriate. The extent to which a question produces a communicative response is less important than the extent to which a question serves its purpose at a particular point in a lesson. In short, the use of appropriate questioning strategies requires an understanding of the *function* of a question in relation to what is being taught.

Compare the two extracts below. In extract 2.3, the teacher is working with a group of low-intermediate adult learners. The class has recently read a story and here, the teacher is simply recapping. It is immediately obvious that the turn-taking, participation and contribution of each learner are all tightly controlled by the teacher's use of display questions.

Extract 2.3

```
 9  T:   I'll see if I have a (2) a photocopy (looks for papers) right you can't find it?
10       look you have this book and cos I've got another book here good … so can you
11       read question 2 Junya
12  L1:  (reading from book) where was Sabina when this happened?
13  T:   right yes where was Sabina? (4) in unit ten where was she?
14  L:   er go out=
15  T:   =she went out yes so first she was in the=
16  L:   =kitchen=
17  T:   =kitchen good and then what did she take with her?
18  L:   =er drug=
19  T:   =good she took the memory drug and she ran OUT
```

In lines 13, 15 and 17, the teacher simply gets students to 'display' what they already know from what they have read. The interaction is rapid and allows little space for full responses, indicated by the latched turns (=). Learner responses are short, typically two or three words and there is no space here for topic development (in lines 14, 16 and 18). We can surmise from this that the teacher's goal was to check understanding before moving on: her choice of display questions here is entirely in tune with her teaching goal. The ensuing IRF sequence highlights the dual function of the teacher's responses: to evaluate a learner response and move the discourse forward with another prompt (in 13, 15, 17).

Compare extract 2.3 with extract 2.4 below. Here, it is immediately evident that learners have more interactional space and freedom in both what they say and when they say it. This is a multilingual group of advanced learners, preparing for a reading activity on the supernatural.

Extract 2.4

49 T: I agree do you do you believe in this kind of stuff? We talked about UFOs and stuff
50 yesterday (2)
51 L: no…
52 L: well maybe …
53 T: maybe no why not? (7)
54 L3: um I'm not a religious person and that's the thing I associate with religion and
55 believe in supernaturals and things like that and believe in god's will and that's so far
56 from me so no=
57 T: I understand so and why maybe Monica?…
58 L4: well I'm also not connected with religion but maybe also something exists but I
59 erm am rather sceptical but maybe people who have experienced things maybe=
60 T: uh huh and what about you [do you]

The teacher's opening question is perceived as a genuine one – he is seeking the opinions of the group. Note the 2-second pause (in line 50) and the relatively short responses by learners in 51 and 52. But it is the question *why not?* in 53, accompanied by the 7 seconds of silence, which promotes the long learner turn in 54. Seven seconds of silence is very unusual in most classrooms; typically, the average wait-time (the length time which elapses between a teacher's question and learner response) is around one second. In line 54, and following 7 seconds of silence, learner 3 produces an elaborated response and works hard to express herself. While to us, as outsiders, the meaning is not immediately apparent, the teacher seems satisfied with her contribution and moves on to another student, Monica, in 57. The teacher's comments (in 53 and 57) are non-evaluative, relating more to the content of the message than the language used to express it. By being non-evaluative, asking genuine questions and allowing pauses, the teacher succeeds in eliciting fuller, more complex responses from the learners and in promoting a more engaged, conversational type of interaction. His choice of questions is extremely important to the resulting extended learner turns and produces a more equal exchange, similar to casual conversation. What these two extracts also illustrate vey nicely is the extent to which classroom discourse is not all of a 'oneness', but a dynamic, constantly shifting series of micro-contexts which are created both through the agenda of the moment and the ensuing interactions (cf. Seedhouse 2004).

2.2.4 Repair

Repair simply refers to the ways in which teachers deal with errors. It includes direct and indirect error correction and the ways in which teachers identify errors in the discourse. Clearly, there is a range of types of error correction available to a teacher at any point in time. As with all strategies, some will be more or less appropriate than others at any given moment. The basic choices facing a teacher are:

(a) Ignore the error completely.
(b) Indicate that an error has been made and correct it.
(c) Indicate that an error has been made and get the learner who made it to correct it.
(d) Indicate that an error has been made and get other learners to correct it.

These choices correlate very closely to the work of conversation analysts who recognise four types of error correction in naturally occurring conversation: self-initiated self repair, self-initiated other repair, other-initiated self repair, other-initiated other repair (see Sacks, Schegloff and Jefferson 1974).

It is apparent when we look at classroom transcripts that error correction occupies a considerable amount of teachers' time. According to van Lier, 'apart from questioning, the activity which most characterises language classrooms is correction of errors' (1988: 276). He goes on to suggest that there are essentially two conflicting views of error correction: one which says we should avoid error correction at all costs since it affects the flow of classroom communication, the other which says we must correct all errors so that learners acquire a 'proper' standard. As teachers, we need to decide on the type and frequency of error correction. Again, the strategies selected must be related to the pedagogic goals of the moment. A highly controlled practice activity requires more error correction than one where the focus is oral fluency. Similarly, there are times in any lesson when errors can be largely ignored and other times when they must be tightly controlled.

It is perhaps also true to say that, within the classroom, learners do expect to have their errors corrected. While it may not be appropriate in more naturalistic settings for speakers to correct each others' errors, in classrooms, this is what learners both want and expect. As Seedhouse puts it, 'making linguistic errors and having them corrected directly and overtly is not an embarrassing matter' (1997: 571). Rather than deciding whether we should or should not correct errors, teachers would do well to consider the appropriacy of a particular strategy in relation to their intended goals. By adopting more conscious strategies and by understanding how a particular type of error correction impacts on the discourse, teachers can do much to tailor their error correction to the 'moment' and promote opportunities for learning.

TASK 2.2

Look at extract 2.5 below. This teacher is working with a group of multilingual adult learners and her stated aim is to elicit feelings and attitudes. In light of this aim, how appropriate is her error correction strategy? What effect does the strategy have on the interaction?

Extract 2.5
11 T: ok does anyone agree with his statement?
12 L: (2) erm I am agree=
13 T: = agree be careful with the verb to agree there you as well Ensa that it's WE
14   agree it's not to be agree it's to agREE Ok=
15 L: oh I agree
16 L: ((3))
17 T: I agree with you but not I AM agree with you the verb is to agree ok so ((3)) to
18   agree with (**writing on board**) is the preposition that follows it I so it's I agree
19   with you I disagree with you … ok em Silvie can you em what were you going
20   to say?
21 L2: I agree with you because em when when we talk about something em for
22   for example you saw a ((2)) on TV=

2.2.5 Student-student interaction

In the current mood of learner-centred teaching and a movement towards learner autonomy, it would seem highly desirable that there should be a movement away from teacher-initiated exchanges towards those instigated by the learner. If teachers are to play a less directive role in the language classroom, they will have to become more facilitative, less dominant and more willing to allow greater equality in the patterns of communication they foster. In the words of Johnson: 'the teacher plays a critical role in understanding, establishing and maintaining patterns of communication that will foster, to the greatest extent, both classroom learning and second language acquisition' (1995: 90).

In light of the considerable disagreement which exists regarding the appropriacy or relevance of a particular theory, it is worth considering some of the optimal conditions for second language acquisition in a formal setting (i.e., in a classroom). According to Ellis (1990), the following conditions must prevail if SLA is to occur optimally:

- Students must have a desire and need to communicate.
- They must be able to play an active role in class, negotiating meaning and making every effort to communicate.
- They should also operate at a level slightly higher than their current language proficiency in a variety of contexts and using a range of language functions.
- Students should be free to self-select and exercise the right to participate in the discourse or remain silent.

Van Lier (1991) characterises similar optimal conditions, but highlights the importance of making students receptive to new language, suggesting that exposure in itself is insufficient. To use Van Lier's terminology, input becomes intake when students are able to make sense of the new language whether based on prior linguistic knowledge or cognitive knowledge. He goes on to describe how intake becomes uptake when learners are able to use the newly acquired language to accomplish an authentic task.

Currently accepted teaching methodologies such as CLT (Communicative Language Teaching) and TBLL (Task-Based Language Learning) emphasise the importance of tasks and stress the need for students to engage in problem-solving activities as a means of developing both linguistic and communicative competence. Clearly, when working with peers, learners have the freedom to self-select, change topic, hold the floor, remain silent in much the same way they have when taking part in everyday conversation. Arguably, in a context where roles are equal and where there is no teacher to direct the interaction, learners should have increased opportunity to acquire the L2. So how effective is student-student interaction and to what extent does it promote SLA?

According to Slimani (1989), when students have control of a topic they are more likely to learn the L2, while Bygate reinforces the centrality of speaking to SLA: 'it is only when the learner is being required to piece together his own utterances that he is being obliged to work out – and hence learn – his own plans of verbal action, all the while evaluating his output in the light of his meaning intention' (1988: 49). Other researchers, however, see student-student interaction as a rather 'impoverished' form of classroom discourse (cf. Rampton 1999), arguing that the linguistic exposure learners get from one another is unlikely to facilitate SLA. Previous studies (see, for example, Porter 1986; Rulon and Creary 1986) compared the interaction of small-group and lockstep (whole class) communication. Their findings are mixed and include the importance of proficiency levels as determinants of interaction, the fact that lockstep teaching may produce more interaction than group-work, and the lack of evidence for interlanguage talk as a determinant of acquisition.

From the discussion so far, it is apparent that the jury is still out concerning the value of student-student interaction in relation to SLA: there is still considerable disagreement among scholars and practitioners. When we look at some classroom data, however, it is immediately obvious that students do benefit hugely from working independently of the teacher, as I hope to demonstrate by looking at extract 2.6 below, where a group of upper-intermediate, multilingual students on a pre-sessional English language course is working independently of the teacher in what might be termed an oral fluency practice activity. They roll a dice and discuss a topic corresponding to the number shown on the dice. If they have already discussed that topic, they simply select another one. What is immediately obvious from the extract is the amount of interactional work that students engage in to keep the discussion moving and on track.

Extract 2.6

1 L1: do you bring his photo with you
2 L3: eh…yeah but we have only a few photos because we get together (.) only one year or
3   so=
4 L2: = and your work was very busy so you have no time to play with him [<L3> Yeah]
5 L1: but I suppose that you must (.) leave some enough money to (.) live with your
6   boyfriend and in this way you can (.) improve the (.) eh ((3)) how do you say=
7 L4: =relationship=
8 L1: =relationship yes [<L4> and know each other]=
9 L3: =yeah I think I now him very well now (laughs) (4) well lets talk another topic=
10 L2: =I remember one thing when they choose register in Coleraine and they organiser
11   know you [reg…register…register]
12 L: [are single girl and they don't know you have a boyfriend
13 LL: ((laugh))
14 L3: I think eh that is is humorous ok he is not very handsome and not very but I think he
15   is very clever ehm and he [<L1> a lot like you] no (laughs) I think he is clever than
16   me and (laughs) (3) he do everything very… [seriously
17 L1:   [seriously
18 L3: yeah ((3)) eh and eh in some eh…in some degree…eh I…admire
19   him (laughs)=
20 L1: = that's a good thing [<L> Yeah] let's change another topic (10)

Students have been asked to talk about pictures of people that they are close to and in line 1 the topic is launched with a question by L1 and an extended response plus justification by L3 in lines 2–3. L2 shows empathy towards L3, making the point that L3 is very busy and has little time to 'play' (sic) with her boyfriend, a point taken up by L1, who says that they can at least live together as a means of improving their relationship. Note how the word search in line 6 is dealt with very quickly by L4 in line 7, allowing the discussion to continue and avoiding a potential breakdown. L4 extends her contribution with an interruption (*and know each other*). The 4-second pause in line 9 indicates an opportunity for a change of speaker or change of topic and this is proposed by L3. However, the change of topic does not occur immediately as L2 interrupts in line 10 with an anecdotal story about registration and the fact that the students doing the registration are able to know who is single.

L2's interruption prompts L3 to conclude her discussion about her boyfriend in lines 14–19 (*he's not very handsome, he's clever and serious about his work*). L1's over-laps are in support of what L3 is saying and offer some kind of affirmation or approval of the comments made by L3. Note too how laughter is used as a way of offering approval and affirmation throughout this extract. Finally, in line 20, L1 brings the discussion back to the original topic switch proposed by L3 in line 9, where there was no switch. Note the extended 10 second pause at the end of the extract, suggesting that the students are considering another topic and that there is now going to be a switch.

This extract is analysed in more detail in Chapter 3 in relation to the construct 'interactional competence'. For our purposes here, suffice it to say that these L2 learners succeed in managing their interaction very well, negotiating meanings, clarifying and managing the topic with no involvement from the teacher. There are no major breakdowns and the discussion flows very well, with each speaker paying close attention to the others, giving appropriate feedback and support as and when necessary.

From this short episode of student-student interaction, it does seem that the benefits of this kind of activity outweigh the shortcomings. Students are more likely to be involved, engaged and challenged when they have opportunities to work together; more importantly, learning opportunities are enhanced and there is a greater likelihood of creating a dialogic classroom atmosphere in which students are free to participate and take risks.

2.2.6 Computer mediated communication (CMC)

In the last twenty years or so, computers have become an essential part of our lives, not only on a personal level, but also on educational and professional levels. This explosion in technology has resulted in huge changes in the ways in which we establish and maintain social relations, go about our personal and professional lives and organise teaching and learning. With the internet now reaching more than 1.6 billion people, there is considerable evidence to suggest that we depend on computer mediated communication to manage our lives (cf. Rosen 2010; Tillema, Dijst and Schwanen 2010), and that social networking is now an essential feature of the lives of young people in particular.

One consequence of the rapid growth of CMC is that technology-enhanced education has also seen an exponential growth, to the point now that traditional definitions of classrooms as physical entities no longer apply. The modern view of a 'classroom' attaches equal importance to its virtual nature as it does to a physical environment where face-to-face teaching takes place. Online and distance learning, blended learning, blogs, virtual learning environments, discussion fora and the like are as much a part of our daily lives as are whiteboards and Powerpoint. While research into the relative merits and shortcomings of CALL (Computer Assisted Language Learning) has been around since the 1970s, relatively little research has been done on the extent to which technology-mediated instruction has benefited learning, nor has there been much research looking at the effects of technology on interaction and learning (notable exceptions include Jenks 2009 and Li 2008). As Jenks (forthcoming) puts it: 'While few researchers and teachers today require a definition of computer, it would not be unfair to say that the full pedagogical potential of current information and communication technologies have yet to be realized.'

The sub-field of applied linguistics which researches the role of technology in classroom interaction is known as CALL-CMC (Computer Assisted Language Learning – Computer Mediated Communication, see Chapelle 2001). Much of this research has adopted what might be called a broadly interactionist perspective (see Long 1996), basing much of its evidence on comparative studies which have looked at the benefits of technology-enhanced communication to learning and teaching. For example, Blake (2007) compares the extent to which CMC leads to the same kind of negotiation for meaning that is normally found in face-to-face interactions. In order to offer a different perspective on CMC in classroom interactions, Jenks calls for more studies which utilise a micro-analytic methodology such as CA to examine, on a turn by turn basis, the nature of CMC in classrooms. Unfortunately, space does not allow a fuller discussion of these issues here and the reader is directed to Jenks (forthcoming) for an up-to-date and comprehensive review of this literature.

In this section, I have described some of the most important features of classroom discourse and illustrated them using data extracts. The features discussed here were teacher's control of the discourse, speech modification, elicitation, repair and student-student interaction. I have tried to show how different strategies are more or less appropriate according to the particular pedagogic goal of the moment and the teacher's understanding of local context.

In the following section, I present a more detailed critique of the prevailing exchange structure which can be found in all classrooms: the three-part IRF exchange structure.

2.3 THE IRF EXCHANGE STRUCTURE

One of the most important features of all classroom discourse is that it follows a fairly typical and predictable structure, comprising three parts: a teacher Initiation, a student Response, and a teacher Feedback, commonly known as IRF, or IRE, Initiation, Response, Evaluation. IRE is preferred by some writers and practitioners to reflect the fact that, most of the time, teachers' feedback is an evaluation of a student's contribution. Teachers are constantly assessing the correctness of an utterance and giving feedback to learners.

This three-part structure was first put forward by Sinclair and Coulthard in 1975 and is known as the IRF exchange structure; it is sometimes also referred to as a recitation script or tryadic structure. The work of Sinclair and Coulthard had a huge impact on our understandings of the ways in which teachers and learners communicate and led to many advances in the field, extending well beyond our understandings of classroom discourse.

An example of the IRF exchange structure is given here:

Extract 2.7

1	Teacher:	So, can you read question two, Junya.	I
2	Junya:	(Reading from book) Where was Sabina when this happened?	R
3	Teacher:	Right, yes, where was Sabina.	F
4	Teacher:	In Unit 10, where was she?	I
5	Junya:	Er, go out …	R
6	Teacher:	She went out, yes.	F

(Walsh 2001)

In this extract, which is typical of teacher-learner interaction and occurs very frequently in classrooms all around the world, we can see how the teacher opens the exchange and marks a new phase of activity with the discourse marker 'so'. This opening remark, or initiation (**I**), leads to the question in line 1, which prompts the student response (**R**) in line 2. In line 3, we see how the teacher offers feedback (**F**) to what the learner has said ('Right, yes'). Feedback is an important feature of the three-part exchange since it allows learners to see whether their response has been accepted or not. Frequently, feedback entails some kind of evaluation, such as *good*, *right*, *ok*.

In line 3, the cycle begins again, with the next initiation ('where was Sabina when this happened?'), which is then clarified in line 4 ('in unit 10, where was she?'). In 5, we see the learner's grammatically incorrect response ('she go out'), followed in 6 by the teacher's feedback and correction. This second IRF sequence follows very logically from the first and was probably followed by a third. Based on this very brief extract, we can make a number of observations about IRF, the most commonly occurring discourse feature in any classroom:

- It enables us to understand the special nature of classroom interaction.
- It enables us to understand why teachers talk so much more than learners: for every utterance made by a learner (**R**), teachers typically make two (**I, F**).
- It allows us to see how, if overused, classroom interaction can become very mechanical, even monotonous. Teachers need to be aware of this.
- While the IRF sequence is both commonly found and appropriate at certain times, there are other types of exchange which are more desirable / useful to learning. We'll come back to this point later.

Sinclair and Coulthard's original work took place in L1 primary classes. Based on recordings of teachers and pupils interacting in class, they produced a hierarchical model for understanding classroom discourse. They found that there were three basic kinds of exchange:

1. Question-and-answer sequences.
2. Pupils responding to teachers' directions.
3. Pupils listening to the teacher giving information.

It is, I believe, fair to say that these basic types of exchange still prevail in the contemporary classroom in many parts of the world. Though there have been some modifications with developments in technology and teaching methods (see above), the IRF exchange still dominates most classroom interaction. Indeed, it can be found in almost any context which uses spoken communication and even in settings where social encounters are mediated by technology. For example, emails and text messages (SMS) often follow a three-part exchange structure. The basic unit of all human spoken interaction, therefore, has three elements: the first, some kind of initiation, is followed by a response and then followed again by some kind of feedback to that response. Most turns-at-talk (or 'moves'), then, are simply a response to a previous contribution.

Consider the example below, taken from a business encounter, in which the interactants, A and B, are talking on the telephone about an invoice:

Extract 2.8

1	A:	What's the last day of the month?	I
2	B:	Friday.	R
3	A:	Friday. We'll invoice you on Friday.	F/I
4	B:	That would be brilliant.	R
5	A:	And fax it over to you.	I
6	B:	Er, well I'll come and get it.	R
7	A:	Okay.	F

The interaction is opened by A in Line 1 with a question (an initiation). B's response in line 2 is then confirmed by A in line 3 (feedback), followed by a second initiation ('we'll invoice you on Friday'). Note how this second initiation is not a question, but still requires some kind of response, which B gives in line 4. Note too how, in everyday communication, the feedback move is optional. B's response in 4 is followed by another initiation by A in line 5, a response by B in 6 and a final follow-up move by A in 7. In everyday settings then, even the most simple, ordinary encounter such as a question and response often has three parts to it and not two as people often think. It is also interesting to note that in the world outside the classroom, responses and follow-ups are not usually reactions to test-questions (speaker A is not testing speaker B on what day it is, unlike the teacher above who was testing the learner's understanding), but show that the speakers have understood one another, and are satisfied with the way the interaction is progressing (*Friday / that would be brilliant / okay*).

For language teachers, understanding the discourse of the classroom itself is crucial, for we teach discourse *through* discourse with our learners. This is another way of saying that in many parts of the world, the main exposure to discourse in English that learners will have is in the classroom itself, via the teacher. A number of studies have compared the discourse of the classroom with 'real' communication (e.g., Nunan 1987). But as van Lier says, 'the classroom is part of the real world, just as much as the airport, the interviewing room, the chemical laboratory, the beach and so on' (1988: 267).

From the early work of Sinclair and Coulthard (1975), we are able to make a number of observations about the nature of classroom discourse and the consequences for learning and teaching. The first observation is that all classroom discourse is goal-oriented. The responsibility for establishing goals and 'setting the agenda' lies largely with the teacher. Pedagogic goals and the language used to achieve them are very closely related, even intertwined. Second, teachers control participation partly through the special power and authority they have, but more importantly, through their control of the discourse. They control who may speak and when, for how long and on what topic. They control turn-taking through the use of IRF; not only do they initiate a response, they offer an evaluation – further evidence of control. A corresponding observation is that learners normally take their cues from the teacher and rarely initiate a response. Their role, one which they are socialised into from a very early age, is to answer questions, respond to prompts and so on. While this is not always the case and there are clearly examples (in university contexts, for example) where learners do take on much more responsibility for managing the discourse, learners normally respond to teachers. Third, we note that the IRF sequence enables us to understand interaction in the classroom, and comprehend its special nature. An awareness of IRF enables us to consider how we might vary interaction more and introduce alternative types of sequence: simply following IRF may result in a rather mechanical, stilted type of interaction. Finally, it is clear that the IRF exchange structure gives us an understanding of the way in which all spoken communication proceeds. This, in turn, has relevance for the ways in which we design tasks and activities for the classroom, highlighting, for example, the need for three- rather than two-part dialogues and emphasising the fact that most spoken exchanges follow this three-part structure.

Both Mehan (1979) and Cazden (2001) studied IRF in great detail and note that it does, in fact, perform a wide range of pedagogical functions which go well beyond the actual confines of the three-part exchange structure as presented by Sinclair and Coulthard in 1975. More recently, other studies have revisited the IRF exchange. Kasper (2001), like Nunan (1987), criticised IRF for its inability to promote genuine communication on a par with that found outside the classroom. Seedhouse (1997) has argued that the kind of discourse which is normally referred to as 'conversation' cannot be replicated in a classroom, which, by definition, is an institutional discourse setting. Other researchers argue that the classroom is a social context in its own right and one which needs to be described and understood like any other context (cf. Johnson 1995; Seedhouse 2004; Walsh 2006).

In the last ten years or so, studies of IRF have tended to focus on the F-move (cf. Cullen 1998; Nassaji and Wells 2000), claiming, like others in mainstream education, that it is at the level of feedback where there is the greatest potential to influence learning (cf. Alexander 2008; Mercer 2009). Some of these studies have drawn heavily on sociocultural theories of learning and it does seem fair to say that making connections between IRF and sociocultural theories of learning holds much promise for future research. There are clear parallels, for example, between sociocultural constructs such as appropriation, affordance, mediation and the 'F' move in the IRF exchange structure. Put simply, a teacher's feedback on a student's contribution is more likely to help learners (cf. scaffolding) and to encourage fuller, more elaborated responses. This discussion will be taken up in some detail in Chapter 3.

2.4 SUMMARY

In this chapter, I have provided a brief sketch of some of the main features of L2 classroom discourse, presented under four main themes: control of patterns of communication, teachers' modified language, elicitation and repair. These themes, or features of classroom discourse, have been chosen because they are representative of the kinds of interaction which typically occur in second language (and other) classrooms. One of the most commonly found structures – the IRF exchange – was then introduced and exemplified. Although it is fair to say that the IRF exchange is still by far the most commonly occurring discourse structure to be found in classrooms all over the world, in later chapters we'll see how its appropriacy can and should be challenged in certain contexts. In Chapter 3, we build on some of these themes by looking at the relationship between classroom discourse and learning and by exploring further the notion of classroom interactional competence (CIC).

Chapter 3

Classroom interactional competence

In this chapter, I present and develop the notion of classroom interactional competence and consider how it can be characterised in different contexts. Classroom interactional competence is defined as: 'Teachers' and learners' ability to use interaction as a tool for mediating and assisting learning' (Walsh 2011: 132). It puts interaction firmly at the centre of teaching and learning and argues that by improving their CIC, both teachers and learners will immediately improve learning and opportunities for learning. Building on many of the ideas put forward in this book and elsewhere, I aim to show how a better understanding of classroom discourse will have a positive impact on learning, especially where learning is regarded as a social activity which is strongly influenced by involvement, engagement and participation; where learning is regarded as *doing* rather than *having* (cf. Sfard 1998; Larsen-Freeman 2010).

The chapter falls into three sections. In the first, we look at the work which has been completed on interactional competence, a construct which has existed for more than twenty years and yet which continues to attract a great deal of attention. In the second section, I characterise classroom interactional competence, using data extracts to examine the strategies open to both teachers and learners to enhance interaction and improve opportunities for learning. In the final section, we consider how teachers might, as part of their professional development, develop their own classroom interactional competence.

3.1 INTERACTIONAL COMPETENCE

One of the most important and central constructs underpinning current language teaching methodologies is *communicative competence*, a term first coined by Dell Hymes in 1972 Communicative competence looks at the ways in which speakers use linguistic, semantic, discourse, pragmatic and strategic resources in order to convey meaning. It has, to a large extent, been a focal point of communicative language teaching and the more recent 'versions' of CLT, broadly couched under task-based language learning and teaching (TBLT).

While communicative competence has certainly furthered our understandings of spoken communication and contributed greatly to advances in language teaching methodology, especially concerning the teaching of speaking, it operates, I suggest, at the level of the individual and focuses on solo performance rather than joint competence. Communication is a joint enterprise which requires collective competence by all parties. Consider any conversation: it is not only the ability of the speaker which is of concern; the listener plays a key role in demonstrating understanding and in clarifying meaning, checking, etc. Essentially, in any conversation (or indeed any spoken interaction), speakers and listeners have equal responsibility to 'make it work' – their ability to do this depends very much on their level of interactional competence, not their communicative competence. We'll come back to this below.

The same is true of language classrooms, where, I suggest, the main concern is individual performance rather than joint competence. Teachers spend a great deal of time assessing and evaluating learners' ability to produce accurate, fluent and appropriate linguistic forms, rather than their ability to interact with another learner or with the teacher. The feedback from teachers is typically at a linguistic rather than interactional level. The same can be said of language testing where, for the most part, the emphasis is on an individual's ability to produce correct utterances, rather than to negotiate meanings or clarify a point of view or idea. Speaking tests focus heavily on accuracy, fluency, grammatical structures, range of vocabulary and so on. They rarely consider how effectively a candidate interacts or how well a candidate co-constructs meanings with another interlocutor. In short, the focus of attention is on individual performance rather than joint competence.

Of course, it is evident that one reason for this position is that a solo performance is easier to teach and easier to test than a joint, collective one. Most teaching and testing materials focus on individual performance and help learners to become more accurate and more fluent; they do not, usually, help learners to become better *interactants* – and yet this is what is needed in the 'real world', where effective communication rests on an ability to interact with others and to collectively reach understandings. Interactional competence, then, is what is needed in order to 'survive' most communicative encounters. Being accurate or fluent, in themselves, are, I suggest, insufficient. Speakers of an L2 must be able to do far more than produce correct strings of utterances. They need to be able to pay attention to the local context, to listen and show that they have understood, to clarify meanings, to repair breakdowns and so on. All of this requires extreme mental and interactional ability, the kind of ability which will not, necessarily, be trained by taking part in pair-work tasks or group discussions.

Against this backdrop, then, lies the notion of interactional competence, first coined by Kramsch as a response against guidelines for language teaching in the USA which emphasised grammatical accuracy over discourse appropriacy. She defined IC as 'the skills and knowledge individuals employ to bring about successful interaction' (1986: 367). Kramsch's main argument is that the focus of language education should be directed towards helping learners to use their existing skills and knowledge to interact by making the focus of attention interactional competence. Kramsch's reference to 'compensating' has resonance with Cook's (2007) notion of a 'deficit' model of foreign language education, where second language speakers are perceived as being in some way inferior to first language speakers, and where the performance of second language speakers is somehow measured against that of first language speakers. More than twenty years ago, then, Kramsch was arguing that a focus on interactional competence would allow teachers to concentrate more on the ability of learners to *communicate* intended meaning and to establish joint understandings. Essentially, interactional competence is concerned with what goes on *between* interactants and how that communication is managed. Rather than fluency, we are concerned with what McCarthy (2005) terms *confluence*: the act of making spoken language fluent together with another speaker. Confluence is highly relevant to the present discussion since it highlights the ways in which speakers attend to each other's contributions and focus on collective meaning-making. It is also a concept that lies at the heart of most classroom communication, where interactants are engaged in a constant process of making sense of each other, negotiating meanings, assisting, clarifying and so on. We might say that, both inside and outside the classroom, being confluent is more fundamental to effective communication than being fluent. In the same way, we might suggest that there is a need to teach interactional competence rather than communicative competence.

More recent studies of interactional competence have looked at the ways in which learners use a range of resources to interact proficiently and participate competently in different L2 encounters. In one of the most comprehensive and convincing recent accounts of interactional competence, Kelly Hall et al. (2011) start from the position that learners, rather than being 'deficient', have a range of interactional competencies which need to be described and understood. Using socially grounded methodologies such as conversation analysis, researchers in this edited collection demonstrate how learners develop interactional competence in a diverse range of contexts and across a number of second languages, including English, German, French, Danish and Icelandic. Other studies, brought together under the sub-discipline now known as CA-SLA (or CA-for-SLA), have considered phenomena such as the influence of task-type on learners' use of interactional resources (Mori 2004), features of participant frameworks between speakers of English and German (Kasper 2004), and the inter-actional resources used by teachers to create learning opportunities (e.g., Hellermann 2005; Koshik 2002; Walsh 2002). All of these studies share a number of perspectives on IC. For example, they emphasise the fact that interactional competence is context specific and concerned with the ways in which interactants construct meanings *together*. They acknowledge, for example, that different interactional resources are needed in a context where the emphasis is on a transaction, such as ordering a coffee, to those required to participate in a multi-party conversation. Clearly, in the first context, a basic knowledge of English will allow you to order a coffee with minimal interactional competence. In the second, however, and in most classroom contexts, much more sophisticated interactional resources will be required if you are to success-fully compete for the floor, gain and pass turns, attend to what the speaker has said, interrupt, clarify and so on. We can see, from these two examples, that interactional competence is highly context specific and related very closely to speaker intent and to audience.

In an attempt to identify specific features of interactional competence, Young (2003) points to a number of 'interactional resources' including specific interactional strategies like turn-taking, topic management, signalling boundaries and so on. Markee (2008) proposes three components, each with its own set of features:

- Language as a formal system (including grammar, vocabulary, pronunciation).
- Semiotic systems, including turn-taking, repair, sequence organisation.
- Gaze and paralinguistic features.

As Markee remarks, developing interactional competence in a second language involves learners 'co-construct[ing] with their interlocutors locally enacted, progressively more accurate, fluent, and complex interactional repertoires in the L2' (2008: 3). It seems that, while this definition does advance our understanding of what IC actually is, it does rely to some degree on more traditional measures of spoken proficiency such as accuracy and fluency. I would even go as far as to suggest that a person who demonstrates a high degree of interactional competence may not be an accurate user of the language, while the converse is also true.

Young offers this definition of interactional competence: 'Interactional competence is a relationship between participants' employment of linguistic and interactional resources and the contexts in which they are employed' (2003: 100). Here then, Young focuses on the relationship between 'the linguistic and interactional resources' used by interlocutors in specific contexts. Clearly, this relationship is an important one and includes, for example, interlocutors' ability to take turns, interrupt politely, acknowledge a contribution, in addition to their ability to make appropriate use of vocabulary, intonation, verb forms and so on. It is the relationship between linguistic and interactional resources which is crucial to effective communication. Consider, for example, the effect of a mis-timed turn or a mis-placed word stress; either can cause 'conversational trouble' and result in the need for repair.

In order to move a little closer to the main focus of this chapter – classroom interactional competence – let's look at some data as a means of developing understandings of interactional competence in a classroom setting. Extract 3.1 below is taken from a pre-sessional English course at a UK university. A small group of multilingual learners, of intermediate ability, are taking part in an oral fluency activity in which they present photographs of important people in their lives and discuss them with their classmates. (For a detailed commentary on the extract, the reader is referred to Chapter 2, where it was first presented.)

Extract 3.1

```
1  L1:  do you bring his photo with you
2  L3:  eh…yeah but we have only a few photos because we get together (.) only one year or
3       so=
4  L2:  = and your work was very busy so you have no time to play with him [<L3> Yeah]
5  L1:  but I suppose that you must (.) leave some enough money to (.) live with your
6       boyfriend and in this way you can (.) improve the (.) eh ((3)) how do you say=
7  L4:  =relationship=
8  L1:  =relationship yes [<L4> and know each other]=
```

```
 9  L3:  =yeah I think I now him very well now (laughs) (4) well lets talk another topic=
10  L2:  =I remember one thing when they choose register in Coleraine and they organiser
11       know you [reg...register...register]
12  L:                [are single girl and they don't know you have a boyfriend
13  LL:  ((laugh))
14  L3:  I think eh that is is humorous ok he is not very handsome and not very but I think he
15       is very clever ehm and he [<L1> a lot like you] no (laughs) I think he is clever than
16       me and (laughs) (3) he do everything very...        [seriously
17  L1:                               [seriously
18  L3:  yeah ((3)) eh and eh in some eh...in some degree...eh I...admire
19       him (laughs)=
20  L1:  = that's a good thing [<L> Yeah] let's change another topic (10)
```

In terms of the interactional competence demonstrated in this extract, we can make a number of observations about the interactional resources employed and their impact on the overall flow and coherence of the discussion:

Turn-taking: It is apparent that all four students manage the turn-taking very well and are able to interrupt, hold and pass turns. Interruptions occur, but naturally and in a supportive way. There are no major breakdowns and the discussion flows well.

Repair: It is interesting to note that even though errors do occur, they are largely ignored. (Cf. lines 1, 2, 4 etc., all containing errors.) This is what Firth (1996) refers to as the 'let it pass' principle; in many business contexts where English is used as a lingua franca, interactants largely ignore errors unless an error causes a problem for understanding. In extract 3.1, the main repair comes in lines 6–8, where the word 'relationship' is needed in order to clarify meaning.

Overlaps and interruptions: Note how overlaps and interruptions occur frequently (for example, in lines 4, 8, 12, 16, 20), but they are supportive and designed to ensure that the interaction flows smoothly. These overlaps and interruptions are examples of what McCarthy (2003) refers to as good 'listenership': they signal to a speaker that she has been understood, that the channels are open and that the communication is working well. Essentially, they 'oil the wheels' of the interaction and help to prevent trouble and breakdowns from occurring. As a deliberate strategy, overlaps give vital clues to speakers that they are being understood and that something is being communicated.

Topic management: One of the key indicators of the coherence of a piece of spoken interaction is topic management and development. In extract 3.1, we can see how the main topic of 'relationships' is introduced, developed and discussed at length despite one attempt to switch topic in line 9 – which is ignored until much later in line 20. Interactants are genuinely engaged with the topic and succeed in maintaining it for some time and from a range of perspectives. In short, we can say that this is a good example of coherent discourse in which all participants are concerned to engage with and develop a topic to the full.

As can be seen from this very brief analysis, an understanding of interactional competence in a classroom setting entails a very different view of both language and learning. We are concerned to develop fine-grained understandings of the ways in which social actions, interactional and linguistic resources combine to create micro-contexts in which understanding and learning can occur. Such understandings can only be attained when we have a clear idea of the context under scrutiny and can relate the actions and interactions of the participants to their intended goals. In relation to extract 3.1, for example, we can make comments on the interactional competence of this group of learners in relation to the extent to which they complete the task or maintain their discussion. In the workplace, or indeed any institutional setting, most tasks entail interaction with others in order to 'get things done' (cf. Drew and Heritage 1992). The business of the moment and the language used to accomplish it are inextricably linked: in a classroom, for example, the teacher's pedagogic goals and the language used to achieve them must work together if learning is to occur. It is this fact which makes it possible to ascertain the extent to which a social encounter in the workplace demonstrates interactional competence: interactional and linguistic resources must work in tandem with the goal of the moment in order to ensure that the business gets done. We return to this later.

At the time of writing, important studies are underway which will contribute to our understanding of interactional competence, both in an educational setting and in more everyday contexts. One such project, *English Profile* (http://www.english profile.org), led by Cambridge University Press, working with a number of partner institutions, recognises that there is much work to be done in terms of characterising interactional competence as the 'fifth skill' (in addition to speaking, listening, reading and writing). It is almost certain that the results of this and related research projects will have enormous implications for language teaching, language testing and materials design. There is certainly likely to be, at the very least, a shift in emphasis towards language as interaction, as a means for communication rather than an academic discipline. Interactional competence is very likely to become the main enterprise of future English language teaching.

TASK 3.1

Thinking about your own context, what do you now understand by interactional competence? What specific features of interactional competence should be developed by both teachers and learners? How would you describe those features?

3.2 CLASSROOM INTERACTIONAL COMPETENCE

Turning now to a conceptualisation of classroom interactional competence, defined here as 'teachers' and learners' ability to use interaction as a tool for mediating and assisting learning' (Walsh 2011: 132), the starting point is to acknowledge the centrality of interaction to teaching and learning. As in any institutional setting, the core business (here, learning a language) is accomplished through interaction; some would even go as far as to say that the interaction which takes place IS the learning – they are one and the same thing (see, for example, van Lier 1988). CIC focuses on the ways in which teachers' and learners' interactional decisions and subsequent actions enhance learning and learning opportunity. In the discussion which follows, together with extracts of classroom data, I present an initial conceptualisation of CIC and consider how this might be used to promote teacher development. Several questions are addressed in the discussion which follows. These include:

1. How do teachers and learners co-construct meaning through interaction?
2. What do participants do to ensure that understandings are reached?
3. How do interactants address 'trouble' and repair breakdowns?
4. What is the relationship between CIC and language learning?
5. How is 'space for learning' created and maintained?

The relevance of CIC is clear. If our aim as language educators is to promote dialogic, engaged and 'safe' classroom environments where learners are actively involved and feel free to contribute and take risks, we need to study the interactions which take place and learn from them. My suggestion here is that we need to acquire a fine-grained understanding of what constitutes classroom interactional competence and how it might be achieved. This can only be accomplished by using data from our own context; the starting point has to be evidence from the classroom in the form of a video or audio recording, self or peer observation. Only by starting to describe inter-actional processes can we begin to understand in some detail our local context. Not only will such an understanding result in more engaged and dynamic interactions in classrooms, it will also enhance learning.

While it is true to say that CIC is highly context specific, not just to the particular class, but to a specific moment in the discourse, there are a number of features of CIC which are common to all contexts. First, teachers may demonstrate CIC through their ability to use language which is both convergent to the pedagogic goal of the moment and which is appropriate to the learners. As mentioned previously, language use and pedagogic goals must work together. Essentially, this entails an understand-ing of the interactional strategies which are appropriate to teaching goals and which are adjusted in relation to the co-construction of meaning and the unfolding agenda of a lesson. This position assumes that pedagogic goals and the language used to achieve them are inextricably intertwined and constantly being re-adjusted (see, Walsh 2006; Seedhouse 2004). Any evidence of CIC must therefore demonstrate that interlocutors are using discourse which is both appropriate to specific pedagogic goals and to the agenda of the moment. This is what I mean by micro-context – micro-contexts (or as I call them *modes*, see Chapter 4) are created through the use of specific interactional features and pedagogic goals which are in turn linked to a particular agenda.

To demonstrate this alignment between pedagogic goal and language use, consider extract 3.2. The data presented here was collected using a stimulated recall methodology (see Chapter 5 for a detailed description); essentially, on the left we see the actual classroom interaction and on the right we have the teacher's commentary on his teaching. The class is of intermediate ability and the students, all adults, are recalling amusing experiences from their school days.

Extract 3.2

1 T: what was the funniest thing that happened to you at school (1) Tang?

2 L1: funniest thing?

3 T: the funniest

4 L1: the funniest thing I think out of school was go to picnic

5 T: go on a picnic? So what happened what made it funny?

6 L1: go to picnic we made playing or talking with the teacher more closely because in the school we have a line you know he the teacher and me the student=

7 T: =so you say there was a gap or a wall between the teacher and the students so when you=

8 L1: if you go out of the school you went together with more (gestures 'closer' with hands)=

9 T: =so you had a closer relationship [outside the school]

10 L1: [yeah yeah]

Basically he's explaining that on a picnic there wasn't this gap that there is in a classroom – psychological gap – that's what I'm drawing out of him. There's a lot of scaffolding being done by me in this monitoring, besides it being managerial, there's a lot of scaffolding because I want to get it flowing, I want to encourage them, keep it moving as it were. I'm clarifying to the class what he's saying because I know in an extended turn – a broken turn – and it's not exactly fluent and it's not articulate – I try to re-interpret for the benefit of the class so that they're all coming with me at the same time and they all understand the point being made by him

A cursory analysis of this extract reveals, I believe, the extent to which this teacher's pedagogic goals and the language used to achieve them are aligned, or working together. Essentially, his comments on the right indicate quite clearly why certain interactional decisions were taken. For example, in the interaction, we see evidence of the teacher constantly seeking clarification, affirming and re-affirming and helping the learner to articulate a full response (in 5, 7 and 9). Each of these responses is designed, according to the teacher, to 'get it flowing' and 'to reinterpret for the benefit of the class'. Not only is he helping the learner to articulate his ideas more clearly, he is helping the rest of the class to understand what is being said. For example, in his own analysis, the teacher refers to the extent to which he uses 'scaffolding' and 'monitoring' as a means of keeping the class together ('so that they're all coming with me at the same time'). He also comments on the need to 'clarify' and 're-interpret' and we see evidence of this in the classroom interaction data: 'so what happened, what made it funny?'; 'so you say there was a gap...'; 'so you had a closer relationship'. This teacher displays CIC from the evidence presented here. It is apparent not only that his pedagogic goals and the language used to achieve them are at one, but also that this teacher knows *why* he has made certain interactive decisions. He is able to articulate quite clearly the interactive decisions taken with this group of learners, a key element of CIC.

A second feature of CIC – and one which, I believe, is common to all language teaching contexts – is the extent to which it facilitates interactional space: learners need space for learning to participate in the discourse, to contribute to class conversations and to receive feedback on their contributions. In short, CIC creates 'space for learning' (Walsh and Li 2013). A brief discussion of what I mean by 'space for learning' now follows before we turn to an example using classroom data.

The starting point for this discussion is to acknowledge the significant developments which have occurred over the last fifteen years or so and which challenge traditional and long-standing views of both the nature of language and the nature of learning. Perhaps the original starting point for these developments was the seminal paper by Firth and Wagner (1997, 2007) which questioned existing conceptualisations of learning, arguing instead that learning should be seen as a social process and that language should be viewed as a complex, dynamic system which is locally managed by interactants in response to emerging communicative needs. It is a view of learning which resonates with much more established sociocultural theories which emphasise its social nature; learners interact with the 'expert' adult teacher 'in a context of social interactions leading to understanding' (Röhler and Cantlon 1996: 2). Learning, under this perspective, entails dialogue, discussion and debate as learners collectively and actively construct their own understandings in and through interactions with others who may be more experienced. This view of learning owes its origins to the influential work of the Russian philosopher Lev Vygotsky (1978), whose theories have been applied to language learning contexts by researchers such as Lantolf (2000) and Lantolf and Thorne (2006).

The work of another sociocultural researcher, Leo van Lier, has considerable relevance to the present discussion. Van Lier's work on ecological approaches to learning (2000) stresses its emergent nature and attempts to explain learning in terms of the verbal and nonverbal processes in which learners engage. If we want to understand learning, we should begin by looking at the interactions which take place; by gaining a closer understanding of these interactions, we are gaining a closer understanding of learning itself. Central to this view of learning is what van Lier terms 'affordance': the relationship between learners and particular features in their environment which have relevance to the learning process. One such affordance in the language classroom is the interaction which takes place between all parties, but especially between teacher and learners. 'Space for learning' in the present context is presented as a specific example of the theoretical construct 'affordance' and my aim is to demonstrate how particular interactional features may create opportunities for learning, or, indeed, influence the learning which takes place. Further, the aim is to demonstrate how teachers can play a pivotal role in creating space for learning by the ways in which they use specific interactional practices and by gaining a closer understanding of the relationship between intended pedagogical goals and the language used to achieve them.

'Learning' here is underpinned by sociocultural theories which emphasise learning as 'doing' rather than learning as 'having' (see, for example, Sfard 1998; Larsen-Freeman 2010). Learning is regarded as a process, an activity, something we take part in, perform. Learning is not something we have or own, it is something which entails encounters with others, where participation is central to the process. There is plenty of evidence to show that learning and participation are closely connected and that participation can support learning (see, for example, Kasper 2004; Mori 2004; van Lier 2000). Under this view, learning is viewed as participation, something that we can measure and track through the interactions which take place (Markee 2008; Hellermann 2008; Pekarek-Doehler 2010). While participation alone cannot be equated with learning, the view taken here is that it affects learning in some way by providing opportunities for reflection and thought (Kasper 2004; Mori 2004). Participation is of considerable relevance to CIC's notion of space for learning, defined here as the ways in which teachers not only create opportunities for participation, but increase student engagement (both at the individual and whole class levels), promote dialogic interaction, enhance affordances by allowing increased wait-time, by paraphrasing and shaping learner responses. This perspective on space for learning, I suggest, offers valuable insights into the learning and teaching process.

There are a number of ways in which space for learning can be maximised. These include increased wait-time, by resisting the temptation to 'fill silence' (by reducing teacher echo), by promoting extended learner turns and by allowing planning time. By affording learners space, they are better able to contribute to the process of co-constructing meanings – something which lies at the very heart of learning through interaction. Note that this does not necessarily mean simply 'handing over' to learners and getting them to complete pair and group work tasks. While this may facilitate practice opportunities and give learners a chance to work independently, it will not, in itself, necessarily result in enhanced learning. The same point has been made by others (cf. Rampton 1999).

What is needed, I would suggest, is a re-thinking of the role of the teacher so that interaction is more carefully understood, and so that the teacher plays a more central role in *shaping* learner contributions. Shaping involves taking a learner response and doing something with it rather than simply accepting it. For example, a response may be paraphrased, using slightly different vocabulary or grammatical structures; it may be summarised or extended in some way; a response may require scaffolding so that learners are assisted in saying what they really mean; it may be recast (cf. Lyster 1998): 'handed back' to the learner but with some small changes included. By shaping learner contributions and by helping learners to really articulate what they mean, teachers are performing a more central role in the interaction, while, at the same time, maintaining a student-centred, decentralised approach to teaching. Several examples of shaping learner contributions can be found in extract 3.2, discussed previously.

Turning now to an illustration of space for learning, let us consider extract 3.3, taken from a secondary English language class in China. This is a large class of around forty students aged 15–16 and of intermediate ability. The class is organised in a 'traditional' way, with students sat in individual desks in rows. Roles too are traditional, and most of the interaction which takes place goes through the teacher. In this extract, the teacher is preparing the class to do a reading activity and is eliciting from them their experiences of visiting museums.

Extract 3.3

```
 1   T:   class begins (3) good afternoon everyone
 2   LL:  good afternoon teacher
 3   T:   sit down please (3) so our topic today is museums (.)
 4        talking about museums (.) have you ever been to museums
 5        (1)? Have you ever been to museums (2)? Yes of course.
 6        And what ↑kind of museums have you been to (4) NAME?
 7   L:   (unclear)
 8   T:   The national museum ↑yes thank you very much and how
 9        about you NAME?
10   L:   (unclear)
11   T:   History museum (.) thank you very much (.) so as you
12        mentioned just now (1) you have been to (puts powerpoint
13        slides of museums up) many kinds of museums (.) but (.)do
14        you still remember ↑when did you go to those museums for
15        the last time (2)? When did you go there for the last
16        time? For example when did you go to the national museum
17        (.) the last time (4)? ((gets microphone from another
18        student)). Thank you
19   L:   er maybe several month ago
20   T:   several month ago thank you ok how about you?
21   L:   I think several years ago
22   T:   several years ago. Ok (laughs). Thank you very much (3)
23        ok actually can you tell me together do you often go to
24        museums?
25   LL:  no
26   T:   No so what you said is just the same as what I read in
27        the newspaper the other day (.) would you please read the
28        title of this piece of news together (points to
29        powerpoint slide)
30   LL:  (reading aloud) why are young people absent from
31        museums?
32   T:   thank you (.) what does it mean? (.) NAME what does the
33        title mean?
34   L:   (.) why young people don't go to museums
35   T:   they don't go to museums very?
36   L:   often
37   T:   very often thank you very much (.) and (.)so actually
```

38		you are young people ↑<u>why</u> don't you go to museums very
39		often(3)? NAME
40	L:	(2) er because erm there's nothing in the museums that
41		er attracts us and er even the mus- things in museums are
42		usually very (.) old
43	T:	old thank you very much ok so nothing can att<u>ract</u> you
44		(writes on blackboard) (3) what else? What else?
45		<u>why</u> don't you go to museums very often? NAME
46	L:	(3) I think going to museums is a wasting of time because
47		because I'm not interested in those old-fashioned things
48	T:	ok thank you very much so you're not in terested in it
49		it's not interesting right? (writes on bb) not
50		interesting (5) ok.

In the extract, a number of interactional strategies are used by this teacher to create space for learning. First, there is evidence of an extensive use of pauses, some of which are quite extensive (lines 1, 3, 6 and 17, for example). This use of 'wait-time' is quite unusual in most classrooms where teachers typically wait for less than one second after asking a question. Here, we see pauses of 2–4 seconds, a feature which has a number of functions:

- It creates 'space' in the interaction to allow learners to take a turn-at-talk.
- It allows thinking or rehearsal time (cf. Schmidt 1993) enabling learners to formulate a response (see lines 44 and 46 where a teacher pause is followed by a learner pause.
- It enables turn-taking to be 'slowed down', helping to make learners feel more comfortable and less stressed.
- Increased wait-time often results in fuller, more elaborated responses, as in lines 40ff and 46ff. It may also result in the kind of dialogic classroom interaction advocated by researchers such as Alexander (2008) and Mercer (2009).

A second strategy used by this teacher to create space for learning is a distinct lack of repair. Although students make some mistakes in this extract (line 34, word order; line 46, verb form 'wasting of time'), they are ignored since they do not impede communication. Importantly, error correction is not the focus of attention in this micro-context where the teacher is concerned to elicit and share personal experiences. A parallel can be found here with the 'let it pass' principle (Firth 1996) whereby, in English as a Lingua Franca (ELF) contexts, interactants often ignore errors which do not impede communication in any way. There is a sense in which the same principle could be considered to be one element of CIC: errors should be corrected as and when necessary and teachers need to move away from a blanket approach under which every error is corrected.

A third feature of space for learning is extended learner turns. In extract 3.3, there are several examples of this feature (in lines 40–42 and 46–47, for example), where the teacher allows learners to complete a turn and make a full and elaborated response. Often teachers interrupt and close down space when learners are attempting to articulate something quite complicated. Here, she does the opposite and allows the student space in the interaction to make a full and useful contribution. Providing the time and space for this to occur are essential; too often teachers may be concerned to move on to the next item on their teaching agenda and may inadvertently interrupt or complete learner turns.

In addition to creating space, in the same extract we can see how space can be 'closed down'. One of the main causes of this is where teachers make excessive use of echo, repeating their own or students' contributions, sometimes with no apparent reason or need. Note that there are two types of echo:

Teacher-learner echo: where a teacher repeats a learner's utterance for the benefit of the class (lines 8, 11, 20 and 22 for example). This is helpful and ensures that a class progresses together and that everyone is 'in the loop'. It is an inclusive strategy which ensures that the whole class comes along together and that there is commonality of understanding (see extract 3.2 where the teacher comments on the need to ensure that the whole class is 'coming with me at the same time'.

Teacher-teacher echo: where a teacher simply repeats her own utterance almost like a kind of habit (lines 4–5, 14–15, 32–33, 44). This serves no real function, arguably, and may impede opportunities for learning since silence can be quite threatening.

The discussion so far has identified two features of CIC: the extent to which language use and pedagogic goals converge, and space for learning. A third feature is what I am calling *shaping*: a teacher's ability to accept a learner's contribution and improve it in some way by scaffolding, paraphrasing, reformulating or extending it. Essentially, through shaping the discourse, a teacher is helping learners to say what they mean by using the most appropriate language to do so. The process of 'shaping' contributions occurs by seeking clarification, scaffolding, modelling, or repairing learner input. In a decentralised classroom in which learner-centredness is a priority, these interactional strategies may be the only opportunities for teaching and occur frequently during the feedback move (cf. Cullen 1998). Elsewhere (see, for example, Jarvis and Robinson 1997), the process of taking a learner's contribution and shaping it into something more meaningful has been termed *appropriation*; a kind of paraphrasing which serves the dual function of checking meaning and moving the discourse forward. Shaping a learner contribution can be compared to what Lyster (1998) calls 'recasting': taking a response, improving it in some way and then 'handing it back' to the learner.

What is evident, both from the discussion here and from previous studies, is that feedback is one of the most important interactional practices a teacher can master since it has the greatest potential to influence learning. The ways in which teachers acknowledge a contribution, evaluate it and make modifications is a skill which requires detailed understanding and practice. All too often, when we look at recordings of teachers, the feedback offered tends to be evaluative, normally comprising a brief comment such as 'thanks', 'right', excellent' and so on. While this kind of feed-back does have its place, more subtle types of shaping are necessary, I suggest, if we are to really help learners communicate their intended meaning. Excessive use of acknowledgement tokens (typically discourse markers such as *right, ok, great, excellent,* etc.) may actually close down an interaction and signal the end of an exchange. This may be both unintentional and undesirable on the part of the teacher; nonetheless, it is what happens in almost all the data I have studied over a number of years.

Looking at the notion of shaping in some data now, we turn to extract 3.4, in which the teacher is working with a group of upper-intermediate learners, studying at a private language school in the UK and preparing to do a listening comprehen-sion about places of interest. There are a number of features in the extract which show evidence of CIC, especially this teacher's ability to manage feedback in a more open and more effective way.

Extract 3.4

1	T:	okay, have you have you ever visited any places ↑outside London?=
2	L1:	=me I stay in (.) Portsmouth and er:: in Bournemouth
3	T:	[where've you been?
4	L1:	[in the south
5	T:	[down (.) here? (pointing to map)
6	L1:	yeah yeah
7→	T:	↑why?
8	L1:	er my girlfriend live here and (.) I like this student
9		place and all the people's young and a lot (.) er go out
10		in the (.) evening its very [good
11	T:	[right
12→	T:	anybody else? (4) Have you been anywhere Tury?
13	L2:	Yes I have been in er (.) Edinbourg ((mispronounced)),
14		(())=
15	T:	=so here here ((pointing to map))=
16	L2:	=yes er Oxford (.) Brighton (.) many places (())=
17	T:	=and which was your favourite?=
18	L2:	=my favourite is London
19→	T:	(.) ↑why?
20	L2:	because it's a big city you can find what what you [want
21	T:	[mmhh
22	L2:	and do you can go to the theatres (1) it's a very (.)
23		cosmopolitan [city
24	L:	[yes
25	L2:	I like it very much=
26	T:	=do you all (.) agree=
27	LL:	=yes (laughter)
28	T:	((3)) laughter)

29	T:	has anybody else been to another place outside London?
30	L:	no not outside inside
31	T:	(.) mm? Martin? Anywhere?
32	L3:	=no nowhere=
33	T:	=would you like to go (.) [anywhere?
34	L3:	[yes yes
35	T:	[where?
36	L3:	well Portsmouth I think it's very (.) great=
37	T:	=((laughter)) cos of the students [yes (.) yes
38	LL:	[yes yes
39	L3:	and there are sea too
40	T:	Pedro?
41	L4:	it's a (.) young (.) place
42→	T:	mm anywhere else? (3) no well I'm going to talk to
43		you and give you some recommendations about where you
44		can go in (.) England (.) yeah

(Carr 2006: DVD 12 task-based learning)

From our knowledge of classrooms and from previous experience, we can ascertain that the teacher's main concern here is to elicit from the students which places of interest they have already visited during their stay in the UK. As a micro-context, the pedagogic goal is to establish a context using students' personal experiences and the main interactional feature is the use of referential (or genuine) questions. One of the most striking features, again, is the lack of repair, despite the large number of errors throughout the extract (see, for example, lines 2, 8, 13, 36, 39), the teacher chooses to ignore them because error correction is not conducive to allowing learners to have space to express themselves. Second, the questions she asks are often followed with expansions such as 'why'? (see, for example, 7, 19) which result in correspondingly longer turns by learners (in 8 and 20). Again, I would suggest that both the teacher's questioning strategy and the longer learner turns are evidence of CIC since they facilitate opportunities for both engaged interaction and learning opportunity. Third, we note that there are several attempts to 'open the space' and allow for wider participation of other learners. This occurs, for example, in 12 (*anybody else* plus a 3-second pause), in 26 (*do you all agree?*), in 42 (*anywhere else* plus a 3-second pause). On each of these occasions, the teacher is attempting to include other students in the interaction in a bid to elicit additional contributions. Again, her use of language and pedagogic goals are convergent, ensuring that learning opportunities are maximised.

Other features which show evidence of CIC include:

- The use of extended wait-time, pauses of several seconds (in 12 and 42) which allow learners time to think, formulate and give a response. Typically, teachers wait less than one second after asking a question (see, for example, Budd Rowe 1986), leaving learners insufficient time to respond.
- The use of requests for clarification (in 3, 5, 15) which serve to ensure that

understandings have been reached. Not only do such requests give important feedback to the students, they allow the teacher to ensure that the other students are included by clarifying for the whole class.

- Minimal response tokens which tell the other speaker that understandings have been reached without interrupting the 'flow' of the interaction (see, for example, 11 (*right*), 21 (*mmhh*). Again, the use of such feedback is further evidence of convergence of pedagogic goals and language use.
- Evidence of content feedback by the teacher, who responds to the message and not the linguistic forms used to articulate a particular message. The teacher responds in an almost conversational way to almost all of the learners' turns. She offers no evaluation or repair of learner contributions, as would be the 'norm' in many classroom contexts. Instead, she assumes an almost symmetrical role in the discourse, evidenced by the rapid pace of the interaction (note the overlapping speech in lines 3–5, 33–35, and latched turns in 14–18 and 25–27).

In the same extract, there are a number of features of CIC which we can highlight from a learner's perspective. First, there is recognition on the part of L1 that the appropriate reaction to a question is a response, the second part of that adjacency pair, as evidenced in lines 2, 4, 6, 8. Not only does L1 answer the questions posed by the teacher, he is able to recognise the precise type and amount of response needed, ensuring that his contributions are both relevant and timely. He is also sufficiently competent to appreciate that a question like 'why' in line 7 almost always requires an extended response, which he provides in 8. His CIC is sufficiently advanced to appreciate that the teacher's focus here is on eliciting personal experiences – while his responses are adequate and appropriate, they are certainly not accurate; yet this is of little or no concern given the pedagogic focus of the moment. This learner has correctly interpreted the teacher's question as a request for further information where accuracy is less important than the provision of that information.

L1 also displays CIC in terms of his ability to manage turns, hold the floor and hand over his turn at a particular point in the interaction. He responds quickly to the teacher's opening question, as indicated by the latched turn in 2 and turn continuation in 4, indicated by the overlapping speech. As well as being able to take a turn and hold the floor, this learner (L1) also recognises key signals which mark a transition relevance place – the teacher's 'right' and accompanying overlap in lines 9 and 10 signal to this learner that it is time to relinquish his turn at talk and hand over to another learner. While it is the teacher who 'orchestrates the interaction' (Breen 1998), nonetheless, L1 has to be able to take cues, observe key signals and manage his own turn-taking in line with what is required by the teacher. He must also recognise that his own contributions are largely determined by the teacher's and by the specific pedagogic goals of the moment.

TASK 3.2

Read the extracts below, the first taken from an ESL class of adult learners in the UK, the second from a senior high school class in China. Based on what you now know about CIC, what features of interactional competence can you identify in each extract? What similarities or differences are there in each of the two contexts?

Extract 3.5(a)
(The teacher is working with a group of elementary adult learners and eliciting information about birthdays as preparation for a pair-work activity.)

```
 1   T: okay let's move on .h (.) there are two questions on the board (.) okay (.) listen to this
 2   one (.) when's your birthday
 3   SS: when's your birthday
 4   T: .h and look at this one (.) what did you get
 5   SS: what did you get
 6   T: what did you get for your birthday
 7   SS: what did you get for your birthday
 8   T: hh good (.) um [S's name] (.) when's your birthday (.) what do you say my birthday's:=
 9   S6: =my birthday's: er (.) thirtieth (.)
10   S: °on°=
11   T: =°okay°=
12   S6: =er on the: thirtieth
13   T: okay good=
14   S6: =°May°=
15   S5: [=°May°=]
16   T:   [on] (.) the thirtieth
17   S6: yeah on the thirtieth May
18   T: of May
19   S6: of May
20   T: °okay° (.) good (.) and (.) your last birthday what did you get (.) did you get money. books.
21   S6: no
22   T: nothing?
23   S6: yes (.) just drink
24   SS: hh hh hh
25   T: just
26   S6: just drink a beer
27   T: just beer
28   S6: yeah (.) hh hh [hh]
```

(Carr 2006, DVD 1: form and accuracy)

Extract 3.5(b)
(The teacher is working with a group of intermediate teenagers aged 15–16 on a reading passage in which they are re-ordering paragraphs in a text.)

```
 1   T:     OK now >would you please< TELL me which paragraphs are the most important
 2           (0.5) which paragraphs are the most important (hand gestures for emphasis) ones (3)
 3           Joe what's your idea
 4   Joe:   (5) er I think it's the first one=
```

```
 5  T:    = you think the first one is  the=
 6  Joe:  =is the most important one
 7  T:    ↑why (.) can you give us [reasons
 8  Joe:                          [er the first paragraph tell tell tells us what what the pass
 9        pass what whole what the whole passage about=
10  T:    =ok thank you interesting idea thank you very much how about the others do you
11        agree with him do you agree with him (3) what about Mei do you also think paragraph
12        1 is the most important part in this passage
13  Mei   yes
14  T:    yes and you have the same reason
15  Mei   yeah
16  T:    ok thank you very much and (0.4) how about the others you can have a discussion
17        with your partners (0.4) which paragraphs are the most impor↑tant in this article
18        (30 seconds. Teacher walks round while students compare their answers in pairs)
19  T:    ok how about Liu
20  Liu   (4) er I think er the last three paragraph is more er is a little bit more important
21        actually er 'cos they introduce the way we get the er get most er young people er or
22        children [interested in museums=
23  T:            [mmhh
24  T:    =↑ok thank you very much
```

In this section, we have seen how CIC might be described and characterised across a range of classroom settings. By studying in some detail the interactions which take place in second language classrooms, we have seen how the interactional and linguistic resources used by both teachers and learners will vary considerably according to specific teaching and learning goals at a particular point in time. Three broad features of CIC were discussed and then analysed in some detail: alignment between pedagogic goals and language use; creating space for learning; shaping learner contributions in feedback. These interactional strategies help to maintain the flow of the discourse and are central to effective classroom communication. They offer a different but complementary view of learning through interaction to that provided by a conversational analytic perspective which focuses mainly on turn design, sequential organisation and repair.

In the final section of this chapter, we consider the ways in which CIC might form the focus of language teacher professional development.

3.3 CLASSROOM INTERACTIONAL COMPETENCE AND TEACHER DEVELOPMENT

TASK 3.3
Thinking about the context in which you either teach English or have studied English, how would you describe CIC? What interactional practices do teachers and learners need? How would you like to change your classroom practices in order to improve CIC in this context?

The broad aim of this section is to suggest ways in which teachers might use the notion of CIC in their own professional development. I have already discussed the ways in which reflective practice might make better use of classroom data in order to help teachers develop fine-grained understandings of their teaching; here I consider how appropriate tools and a more sophisticated use of terminology (or metalanguage) can be used to enhance understandings of classroom interaction in the development of CIC.

The discussion which follows outlines a number of ways in which teachers can develop CIC by making their changes to practice data-led.

3.3.1 Multiple methods, multiple perspectives

One of the most important principles of any class-based research is the need for evidence which reflects more than one perspective and which utilises more than one methodology. For example, in order to enhance understandings of interactional practices, teachers might use recordings, interviews, stimulated recall procedures, observation, introspective journals and so on. Obtaining multiple perspectives on the same context provides a rich and detailed description which might reveal evidence which was previously unseen. Central to this process is the endeavour to obtain an 'emic' or insider account of what happens in classrooms. For example, stimulated recall (see below) has the advantage of presenting voices and actions side by side, giving a comprehensive representation of both the classroom discourse and teachers' perspectives on the interaction. The advantage of this approach is that it presents a lifelike portrayal of classroom life and includes the commentary of one of the actors. Under a 'perspectival' (Maykut and Morehouse 1994: 20) description of L2 classroom interaction like the one proposed here, issues of subjectivity and objectivity become less pertinent in the search for an honest, insider account. Actions, events, reactions and comments can be presented side by side enabling teachers to make more informed decisions concerning future changes to practice.

Using multiple methods of data collection permits both closer scrutiny of the constructs and greater confidence in the findings, as well as exposing teachers to different means of professional development. Just as language learners need to be involved in different types of classroom activity to compensate for different learning styles and preferences, so too practitioners benefit from the use of a range of reflective practices and instruments in order to reflect preferred ways of attaining professional development (see also Shaw 1996). In addition, the different narrative styles and reporting foci of respondents can be appropriated when multiple methods of data collection are used. Differences in interviewee style, the fact that one teacher is more vocal than another, or that some teacher-participants have a tendency to be overly critical of their class performance can all be compensated by using multiple methods, a viewpoint previously advanced by Block (1996: 192).

3.3.2 Untranscribed lesson recordings

One of the most daunting features of research on classroom interaction is that of transcription. It is perhaps one of the main reasons why second language teachers do not engage in professional development activities which are based on recordings and transcripts of their teaching. Here, I argue that much can be achieved *without* transcribing, and that there is considerable merit in using untranscribed audio or video recordings.

While action research clearly has much to offer in terms of the potential it provides for professional development, many teachers simply do not have the time or energy to reflect on their teaching (van Lier 1996), partly because they do not have the time to engage in wholesale transcription of their lessons. According to Allwright and Bailey (1991: 62), one hour of class-time can take up to 20 hours to transcribe. Rather than transcribe, then, I am proposing that teachers should be given some kind of tool or framework which helps them to focus on particular aspects of their teaching. The SETT framework (see Chapter 4) is one such instrument which falls under the *ad hoc* self-observation scheme advocated by researchers like Wallace (1998). It allows self-observation and analysis, but avoids wholesale transcription.

The principal advantages of using untranscribed recordings are summarised below:

- Microscopic analysis is, arguably, more feasible when specific instances of a particular feature are identified since attention is drawn to when and how that particular feature (for example, display question) is used. By 'noticing' how specific interactional practices are used, teachers build up a profile of their verbal behaviour and are better equipped to make changes.
- Short extracts from a recording permit extended discussion during reflective feedback interviews; longer stretches of discourse become more difficult to analyse, since underlying patterns are lost in the discourse.
- A 15-minute lesson extract can be analysed in 45–50 minutes when only one or two features are being investigated. A full transcript of a whole 50-minute lesson might take 4–5 hours.
- Because the process is repeated, a wider range of lesson-types can be analysed over a relatively short period of time. The aim is to collect short recordings (see below) and study how different interactional features are employed.
- The perspective is that of the teacher rather than an outside researcher: understanding of the interaction is derived from the inside, allowing smaller amounts of data to be utilised.
- Lengthy transcription necessarily entails reduction and idealisation; the use of shorter extracts, in which the actor and researcher are one and the same person, is more likely to present a faithful recording of 'what really happened' (Edwards and Westgate 1994).

3.3.3 'Snapshot' lesson extracts

Again, much can be learnt from what I am calling 'snapshot recordings', lasting 10–15 minutes and taken from different stages of a series of lessons. Again, providing teachers have a clear focus and know what they are studying, short, partial extracts of lessons can be equally valuable in sensitising teachers to their interactive decision-making. Arguably, there is more to be gained from repeated analysis of partial lessons than one analysis of a single lesson, particularly if recordings are taken from different classes and at different times in a lesson. Many of the studies adopting reflective practice principles have involved teachers in a *single* instance of reflection: one interview, one lesson observation, one stimulated recall procedure (see, for example, Bailey 1996; Tsui 1996; Thornbury 1996). It is, from a teacher development perspective, certainly more advantageous to aim for instances of *multiple* reflective practice, using a different 'snapshot' on each occasion. Like most new skills, reflective practices can be honed through repetition; the use of short extracts offers repeated practice and provides teachers with an opportunity to notice different aspects of their interactional practices.

Arguably, a fine-grained treatment of a relatively small amount of data, following a specific procedure which is repeated, is more likely to foster awareness than more complex analyses of longer transcripts. The advantage of lesson 'clips' is that a variety of contexts is encountered, permitting comparison of the interactional organisation of different classes: levels, nationalities, class composition, lesson types and teaching aims can be contrasted and recurrent patterns identified. In addition, teachers are free to select which part of a lesson to use.

3.3.4 Stimulated recall procedures

As a procedure for second language teacher development, stimulated recall has much to commend it, offering, as it does, the potential for interaction and interactive decision-making to be compared simultaneously. The voices and actions of teachers can consequently be analysed side by side, offering a multi-layered, fine-grained and emic perspective on any teaching encounter. In its most straightforward form, stimulated recall involves making a recording, analysing it and then commenting on particular issues as they arise, usually with another colleague or trusted 'critical friend' (for a full account see Lyle 2003). Although the procedure was originally intended to help participants recall and explain past actions, it is a very useful means of accessing the complex practices and procedures which make up teaching. It provides a springboard for discussion and supplies the evidence needed to make informed judgements. One of the most productive uses of stimulated recall is as a means of examining the decisions made by teachers as they teach, a phenomenon which I am calling 'online decision-making' (Walsh 2006).

Other researchers have studied the decisions taken by teachers as they teach, commenting on the relative values of those choices in influencing interaction (see, for example, Woods 1989; Westerman 1991; Johnson 1992). Based on the evidence from these and other studies, the 'planfulness' (Leinhardt and Greeno 1986: 75) of teacher's decision-making represents only one aspect of skilled teaching; current and future research needs to understand what lies behind decisions taken online in order to better inform interactive choices and enhance interactional processes. When viewed as an interactive decision-making process, much professional development can be encouraged in terms of promoting understandings of what lies behind decisions taken. For example, a teacher may suddenly launch into a lengthy grammar explanation in the middle of engaging students in a discussion – explaining this action might be extremely developmental.

In a previous study (Walsh 2006), eight teachers took part in a four-stage stimulated recall procedure which entailed a video recording of one complete (50-minute) lesson by each teacher-participant. This recording was then viewed by the teacher and one colleague and their comments on interactional practices were recorded in an audio recording. The third step involved the same group of teachers evaluating their verbal behaviour in the light of intended learning outcomes. Finally, the interviews were recorded, analysed and compared with the original video recording, enabling actions and comments on actions to be compared.

To summarise, the main advantages of stimulated recall are:

- It offers scope for clarification and question and comment generation on classroom interaction as it unfolds. Misunderstandings can be eradicated, ensuring that a common perspective on the discourse is attained.
- The commentary and accompanying interaction are extremely transparent. There is considerable richness in the presentation of the data, including the potential for checking and cross-checking of 'reality'.
- There is considerable scope for raising awareness since fine-grained analysis of the interaction is possible and there is the potential for repeated playback and reviewing.

TASK 3.4

The following is an extract from a stimulated recall procedure. Look at the classroom interaction (on the left) and the teacher's commentary (on the right). In what ways might we say that this teacher shows evidence of CIC, either in the actual teaching or in the follow-up comments? How might you use stimulated recall in your own context?

Extract 3.6
Students are preparing to do a board game and clarifying vocabulary
(15 minutes)

L: what does it mean singe, singed my   *What I liked about this is that they*
eyebrows?   *were all asking questions. So for me,*

T: singed, singed (**writes on board**)
(4) to singe means really to burn but
it always has the sort of the meaning
to burn something with hair=
L: =some people you know too close
to the fire so it singed your eyebrows
burns your eyebrows
T: yeah, yeah
L: (12) bump into cupboard door is
it like hit?
T: yeah it's like knock into
L: (20) fractured means like twist
T: no fractured [means broken]
L:　　　　　[broken] (12)

that would point up the use of
providing a structured type of activity;
although there's a lot management
time setting it up, because they know
they've got that time, they'll play a far
more active role in it. So again,
shutting up and letting them get on
with it.

3.4 SUMMARY

In this chapter, I have presented and characterised the construct 'classroom inter-actional competence'. Placing interaction at the centre of learning, I have argued that in order to enhance learning and learning opportunity, teachers should begin by developing their own interactional competence. While I suggest that classroom inter-actional competence is highly context specific (both in the general social / geographic sense and in the more specific sense of 'context of the moment'), there are certain features of CIC which can be encouraged and promoted in any setting. By adopting specific interactional strategies, CIC can be greatly enhanced. These strategies include the need for teachers to create space for learning, the importance of jointly created understandings, the value of shaping learner contributions, the need to engage and involve learners in dialogue and so on.

Clearly, it is important for teachers to decide for themselves how to improve their CIC. What I have attempted to do in this chapter is to offer some thoughts on the various elements which make up CIC and suggest how teachers might enhance their own understandings. Like all professional development, there is no one 'right way' to improve. However, understanding a specific context and developing skills appro-priate to that context are central to any endeavour towards becoming a better teacher. Developing an understanding of classroom interaction and improving the way that interaction is managed are, I suggest, central to improving teaching.

Chapter 4

SETT: self-evaluation of teacher talk

In the last chapter, I presented the construct 'classroom interactional competence', characterised across a range of contexts. The chapter concluded with a discussion about how CIC might become the focus of second language teacher professional development, using the argument that teachers need some kind of evidence in order to make changes to their professional practice. In this chapter, I present a framework (SETT: self-evaluation of teacher talk) designed in collaboration with L2 teachers and which aims to foster teacher development through classroom interaction. Essentially, my aim is to get teachers to think about classroom interaction as a means of improving both teaching and learning. (For a fuller discussion of this work, see Walsh 2006). This framework is one example of the kind of 'tool' which I believe to be central to reflective practice and teacher development; it can be regarded as an example of an *ad hoc* self-observation instrument similar to that advocated by researchers like Wallace (1998). Essentially, the argument is that by using appropriate tools, teachers can gain the kind of fine-grained, up-close, 'ecological' (van Lier 2000) understanding of their local context. An understanding of context lies at the heart of professional development and is, arguably, the first step towards enhancing learning and teaching.

The SETT framework has been used in a range of educational settings since its publication in 2006. These include initial teacher education programmes (PGCE) for English and Drama teachers (Walsh and Lowing 2008); INSET courses for experienced teachers; a study evaluating the value of classroom observation in the Middle East (Howard 2010); on CELTA programmes around the world; a primary science classroom; various secondary EFL contexts around the world; two university classroom contexts, and an Irish medium secondary classroom. In short, the framework has been used extensively to promote awareness and understanding of the role of interaction in class-based learning and to help teachers improve their practices.

The SETT framework comprises four classroom micro-contexts (called *modes*) and thirteen interactional features (called *interactures*). Classroom discourse is portrayed as a series of complex and inter-related micro-contexts, where meanings are co-constructed by teachers and learners and where learning occurs through the ensuing talk of teachers and learners. In the remainder of this chapter, the framework is presented and evaluated, beginning with a discussion about context and micro-contexts.

4.1 CONTEXT AND CONTEXTS

TASK 4.1

As teachers, we spend a lot of time highlighting the importance of context. What are the most important features of context for you? Which features can you influence and which are fixed?

Language teachers, teacher educators and researchers constantly make reference to 'real world' contexts, which can be found, it seems, somewhere outside the classroom. The 'real world' is the place where we use language for 'real' communication. In contrast, and by logical deduction, the language classroom is the place where we engage in communication which is somehow not 'real', but contrived, artificial. There is even a sense in which this 'unreal' context is somehow inferior or deficient to the one found 'out there', and a view that if we want to learn a language, we must get into this real world. This situation has prevailed for many years and it is clearly both misleading and untrue: the language classroom is as much a 'real' social context as any other and should be viewed as such. What takes place in a classroom is as real and authentic as what takes place outside – it is a genuine context in which we engage in real communication and interaction.

According to Drew and Heritage (1992), much of the research on L2 classroom interaction to date has adopted an approach whereby context is viewed as something static, fixed and concrete. The majority of studies have had one of two central goals, attempting to account for either the nature of verbal exchanges, or the relationship between SLA and interaction (Wu 1998). Whatever their focus, most studies have referred to *the* L2 classroom context (singular), implying that there exists such an entity and that it has fixed and describable features which are common to all L2 contexts. One possible explanation for this is the over-riding concern of both practitioners and researchers to compare L2 classroom interaction with 'real' communication. By following this line of enquiry, many researchers have failed to acknowledge that the classroom is as much a 'real' context as any other situation in which people come together and interact.

Van Lier's more recent work (2000) considers classroom interaction from a variable perspective, arguing that the L2 classroom can be compared to a natural environment; if we change one element of a natural environment, it will have consequences somewhere else. We only have to consider the effects of climate change on the world we live in today to understand this position. In his 'ecological' perspective on context, van Lier makes a similar observation: a classroom environment is constantly shifting and we need to focus more on the different interactional processes at work in order to understand that environment. He draws parallels with natural science, where any changes to one species may affect another one. Other writers have proposed that classroom interaction should be investigated from a multi-layered perspective, where participants play a crucial role in constructing the interaction and under which different varieties of communication prevail as the lesson unfolds according to particular pedagogic purposes (see, for example, Johnson 2009; Lantolf 2000; Seedhouse 2004; Tsui 1994).

The one thing that all these studies (and there are many more) have in common is that they advocate a *variable* view of classroom context. It is a perspective which is based on a number of assumptions which are both widespread and common to almost any teaching and learning environment. The first assumption is that all L2 classroom discourse is goal-oriented, as is the case with most institutional discourse. Related to this observation is the fact that roles are asymmetrical and the prime responsibility for establishing and shaping the interaction lies with the teacher (Johnson 1995). A third and crucial assumption is that pedagogic goals and language use are inextricably linked (Cullen 1998; Seedhouse 2004): classroom interaction unfolds according to the pedagogic goal of the moment and the language used to realise that goal.

The main advantage of a variable perspective is that it offers a more realistic interpretation of what's actually happening in classroom discourse. In particular, there is the recognition that interaction patterns do and should vary according to the different agendas and social relationships of the participants and according to the linguistic and pedagogic purposes of the teacher. Any analysis of classroom interaction should take account of the fact that those patterns are dynamic and mutually constructed by the participants, not static and pre-determined. The notion of a single context is invalid and unworkable; rather, we need to view classroom interaction as a series of contexts, plural.

Several writers have adopted a variable approach to the study of classroom discourse, each proposing a number of micro-contexts. For example, van Lier (1988) identifies four types of second language classroom interaction, each one organised according to the emphasis placed on topic or activity and according to whether the discourse is tightly or loosely controlled. While it is unlikely that van Lier's classification is exhaustive and capable of accounting for all types of interaction, it is certainly representative of the typical patterns which occur and makes some attempt to relate language use to classroom practice.

A more recent variable approach to the study of classroom discourse is the one advocated by Kumaravadivelu, which uses what he terms Critical Classroom Discourse Analysis (CCDA) aimed at 'understanding what actually transpires in the L2 classroom' (1999: 453). The concern of this framework is to develop understandings of the sociolinguistic, sociocultural and sociopolitical dimensions of classroom discourse by recognising that all interactions are located socially, temporally and historically. Understanding 'what really happens' in the classroom needs to take account of the voices, fears, anxieties and cultural backgrounds which result in the commonly found mismatches between 'intentions and interpretations of classroom aims and events' (1999: 473). Essentially, what Kumaravadivelu is arguing is that an understanding of classroom interaction requires an awareness of what participants bring to a classroom, in terms of their beliefs, attitudes, knowledge, expectations, conditioning and so on, as well as what actually goes on in the classroom. Howard (2010) terms these external factors (what participants bring) and internal factors (what actually happens). Clearly, any interaction is determined by a complex mix of external and internal factors.

Looking more at the specific details of classroom interaction from a conversation analytic perspective, Seedhouse (2004) characterises the 'interactional architecture of the second language classroom' by studying the turn-taking and sequentiality of L2 classroom discourse. His study identifies six micro-contexts, each with specific inter-actional features and pedagogic goals which distinguish one from another. The main contribution of this work is that it clarifies the relationship between pedagogic goals and the language used to realise them and demonstrates the ways in which classroom discourse is made up of a series of micro-contexts. To some extent this is true of each of the studies reviewed here: contexts are created by teachers and learners as they engage in face-to-face interaction and according to teachers' pedagogic goals at a given moment. Classroom interaction is therefore socially constructed *by* and *for* the participants, leading some writers to suggest that we should think of learning 'as a process of becoming a member of a certain community [necessitating] the ability to communicate in the language of this community and act according to its particular norms' (Sfard 1998: 6). A variable approach to the study of L2 classroom contexts, by focusing more on participation, enables greater understanding of 'language socialization' (Pavlenko and Lantolf 2000: 156).

Another feature of a variable approach to classroom discourse is the emphasis given to the important relationship between language in interaction and learning. An understanding of the relationship between classroom communication and edu-cational goals, the ways in which language use can facilitate or hinder learning (Walsh 2002), has implications for teacher development, replacing 'broad brush' views of interaction with fine-grained paradigms which permit greater understanding of the interactional and learning processes at work. By looking at longer stretches of discourse and by considering the relationship between language use, pedagogic goals and learning opportunities, it is possible to obtain a more complete understanding of 'what is happening' in the discourse.

One of the problems of the studies reviewed here is that there is no commonly agreed metalanguage used to discuss micro-contexts and interactional features, making comparisons difficult and replication of studies almost impossible. As Walsh puts it: 'Description and understanding of L2 classroom interaction is unlikely to be advanced until [a metalanguage] is identified and utilized by teachers and researchers alike' (2011: 67). One of the aims of this chapter is to provide such a metalanguage and to offer a tool which can be used for professional development. In the next section, I present an overview of the SETT framework.

4.2 THE SETT FRAMEWORK

The SETT framework (Walsh 2006) was designed as a means of helping teachers gain a closer understanding of their local context, describe the classroom interaction of their lessons, and develop an understanding of interactional processes – all with the ultimate goal of improving learning and teaching. As we have seen in the previous section, the backdrop to SETT is that classrooms are made up of multiple contexts which are locally constructed by teachers and learners. The notion of 'the L2 lesson context' is too general; 'contexts are locally produced and transformable at any moment' (Drew and Heritage 1992: 19). When considering interaction in the classroom, therefore, we need to acknowledge that classroom discourse comprises a series of micro-contexts, linked to a range of 'external' factors (cf. Howard 2010) such as beliefs, attitudes, previous experience and so on. These micro-contexts are created in and through the interaction, which is also the way in which meanings are co-constructed (cf. Lantolf and Thorne 2006). The relationship between language use and pedagogic goals requires closer understanding (cf. Seedhouse 2004).

From this introduction, it is clear that pedagogy and interaction cannot be separated – they are interdependent. Using the term *mode* encompasses the interrelatedness of language use and teaching purpose. A mode is defined as 'an L2 classroom micro-context which has a clearly defined pedagogic goal and distinctive interactional features determined largely by a teacher's use of language' (Walsh 2006). The definition is intended to emphasise the idea that interaction and classroom activity are inextricably linked, and to acknowledge that as the focus of a lesson changes, interaction patterns and pedagogic goals change too.

In the 2006 study, Walsh set out to design a framework which could be used by teachers to evaluate and gain closer understandings of the interactions taking place in their classes. The work was conducted in a UK university's English Language Centre and the participants were the tutors and students of that centre. Recordings were made and analysed using an applied conversation analysis methodology (ten Have 2007). To summarise, the following procedures were followed:

- The total size of the corpus is approximately 100,000 words, or 12 hours.
- Data were analysed using an applied CA methodology.
- Participants were invited to study the transcripts in a series of workshops in which the precise focus of each lesson was discussed in relation to pedagogic goals.
- Interaction patterns were found to vary according to instructional activity; for example, establishing procedures to complete an activity resulted in a very different pattern of interaction to open-class discussion.
- The different patterns manifested themselves in the turn-taking, sequence of turns and topic management. Once a pattern had been identified, the data were analysed for further examples of the same pattern as is the 'norm' under conversation analysis (Psathas 1995: 52).
- Following this procedure, four patterns, four micro-contexts, were identified. These were called *modes*: managerial mode, classroom context mode, skills and systems mode, materials mode.

Each mode is made up of specific interactional features (such as display questions, repair, content feedback) and particular pedagogic goals. The four modes are included as being representative, rather than comprehensive, and can be adapted to suit local contexts. They are based on the analysis of frequently occurring classroom discourse features and are designed to help teachers develop detailed understandings of their own contexts.

A parallel to this study is the work of Heritage and Greatbach (1991), whose notion of 'fingerprints' is helpful to the present discussion. In their study, the researchers identified a number of socially constructed contexts in different institutional settings which they term 'fingerprints' to differentiate interactional organisations from one workplace to another. Thus, the 'fingerprint' of a doctor's surgery will have a different exchange and participation structure to that of a solicitor's office. Following Heritage and Greatbach, under SETT, each L2 classroom mode has its own distinctive fingerprint, comprising pedagogic and linguistic features. Thus, the fingerprint of *classroom context* mode is markedly different to that of *managerial* mode; both are different again from *skills and systems* mode.

The four modes, together with their interactional features and typical pedagogic goals, are summarised in Table 4.1.

Table 4.1   L2 Classroom Modes (Walsh 2006)

Mode	Pedagogic Goals	Interactional Features
Managerial	• To transmit information • To organise the physical learning environment • To refer learners to materials • To introduce or conclude an activity • To change from one mode of learning to another	• A single, extended teacher turn which uses explanations and/or instructions • The use of transitional markers • The use of confirmation checks • An absence of learner contributions
Materials	• To provide language practice around a piece of material • To elicit responses in relation to the material • To check and display answers • To clarify when necessary • To evaluate contributions	• Predominance of IRF pattern • Extensive use of display questions • Form-focused feedback • Corrective repair • The use of scaffolding
Skills and systems	• To enable learners to produce correct forms • To enable learners to manipulate the target language • To provide corrective feedback • To provide learners with practice in sub-skills • To display correct answers	• The use of direct repair • The use of scaffolding • Extended teacher turns • Display questions • Teacher echo • Clarification requests • Form-focused feedback

Classroom context	• To enable learners to express themselves clearly • To establish a context • To promote oral fluency	• Extended learner turns • Short teacher turns • Minimal repair • Content feedback • Referential questions • Scaffolding • Clarification requests

In the following sections, a description of each mode, together with examples from the data, is presented.

4.2.1 Managerial mode

Managerial mode is an 'enabling mode' (McCarthy and Walsh 2003) which both explains and details the ways in which learning is organised. Its main pedagogic goal is to locate learning in time and space and to set up or conclude classroom activities. It frequently occurs at the beginning of lessons, as illustrated in extract 4.1, characterised in the first instance by an extended teacher turn of more than one clause and a complete absence of learner involvement.

Extract 4.1

T: OK we're going to look today at ways to improve your writing and at ways which can be more effective for you and if you look at the writing which I gave you back you will see that I've marked any little mistakes and eh I've also marked places where I think the writing is good and I haven't corrected your mistakes because the best way in writing is for you to correct your mistakes so what I have done I have put little circles and inside the circles there is something which tells you what kind of mistake it is so Miguel would you like to tell me one of the mistakes that you made (3)

In this extract, the focus is on the 'institutional business' of the moment, the core activity of the school, organisation or whatever. In managerial mode, there are frequent repetitions, directives and instructions. Here, we see how the teacher helps learners to 'find their place', summarising previous actions and getting students 'on the same page'. At the end of managerial mode, there is typically a handing over to learners and a movement into another mode – in this extract, for example, the words 'so Miguel' act as a transition to another mode, here, skills and systems. Note too the use of discourse markers such as *ok, so, now, right*, etc., which help learners to follow what is being said and give direction to the discourse. Once learning has been located, learners are invited to participate: *so Miguel, would you like to tell me one of the mistakes that you made*. Locating learning is an important first step in building a main context; consequently, in many respects, managerial mode functions as a support to the other three modes.

Although it is most commonly found at the beginning of a lesson, managerial mode may occur post-activity or as a link between two stages in a lesson, as indicated in extract 4.2 below, where the teacher's aim is to conclude an activity and move the lesson on. As in the previous extracts, turn-taking is wholly managed by the teacher, learners have no interactional space, and the agenda, the pedagogic goal of the moment, is firmly in the hands of the teacher. Once the activity is concluded, the learners are organised into three groups and the lesson moves from one type of learning (pair-work practice) to another (open class checking in groups). Throughout, the teacher's use of language and pedagogic purpose are at one: the language used is appropriate to the pedagogic goal of the moment.

Extract 4.2

T: all right okay can you stop then please where you are ... let's take a couple of ... examples for these and ... put them in the categories er ... so there are three groups all right this one at the front Sylvia's group is A just simply A B and you're C (teacher indicates groups) all right so ... then B can you give me a word for ways of looking (3) so Suzanna ... yeah

The transition markers *all right, okay, so* signal the end of one part of the lesson and alert learners to the fact that the lesson has moved on, that pedagogic goals have been realigned with a shift in focus to a new activity. These discourse markers are essential for learners to follow the unravelling interaction and 'navigate their way' (Breen 1998) through the classroom discourse. They function like punctuation marks in a written text, or intonation patterns in a spoken text and are crucial to understanding. In cases where discourse markers are not used, the boundaries between modes are difficult to detect and learners may become confused as to what they are expected to do.

To summarise, managerial mode is characterised by one, long teacher turn, the use of transition markers and an absence of learner involvement. Its principal pedagogic purpose is the management of learning, including setting up a task, summarising or providing feedback on one particular stage of a lesson. It typically occurs at the beginning or end of lesson, or at the beginning or end of a particular activity.

4.2.2 Materials mode

In this mode, pedagogic goals and language use centre on the materials being used. All interaction typically evolves around a piece of material such as a text, tape, worksheet, or course-book. In most cases, the interaction is tightly controlled and follows the IRF exchange structure. That said, the degree of control exercised by the teacher may be relatively tight or loose, as evidenced in extracts 4.3 and 4.4 below.

Extract 4.3

1 T: I'll see if I have a (2) a photocopy (looks for papers) right you can't find it? look you
2   have this book and cos I've got another book here good ... so can you read question
3   2 Junya
4 L1: (reading from book) where was Sabina when this happened?

5	T:	right yes where was Sabina? (4) in unit ten where was she
6	L:	er go out=
7	T:	she went out yes so first she was in the=
8	L:	=kitchen=
9	T:	=kitchen good and then what did she take with her?
10	L:	=er drug=
11	T:	=good she took the memory drug and she ran OUT … very good question 3 can you
12		read er?=
13	L2:	=er where was the drug? … in the bag
14	T:	(laughs) sorry?
15	L2:	where where was the drug?=
16	T:	=and you answered in the bag (laughs) very good …

While both extracts can clearly be categorised as materials mode because the interaction flows from the material, there are striking differences. In extract 4.3, the teacher's pedagogic purpose is to review a previous unit in the course-book before watching a video clip. The interactional patterning is tightly controlled; turns are latched, following on from each other very closely (indicated by = in the transcript), the topic is determined by the material, and the teacher elicits, evaluates and displays learner responses, correcting and extending their contributions at lines 7, 11 and 16. The sequencing of turns follows very closely the IRF exchange structure (Sinclair and Coulthard 1975), with the teacher controlling participation very tightly by initiating (I) a learner response (R) and then offering feedback (F), normally in the form of an evaluation. In light of the teacher's pedagogic goals, we might say that this rapid-fire question-response-evaluation sequencing is entirely appropriate: pedagogic goals and language use are convergent.

In extract 4.4, on the other hand, we see a very different type of turn sequencing. Here, a group of pre-intermediate students is working on a fluency practice activity using *Harrap's Communication Games* and a task called 'Good news, bad news'.

Extract 4.4

1	L1:	was shy so didn't have a ((1))=
2	L:	so it's good news (laughter)
3	LL:	/bad news/ ok / no no that's good news/…
4	L2:	bad news …
5	L:	no that's bad news=
6	L3:	=ah good good news (2)
7	L1:	no no that's wrong you have to do bad news …
8	L2:	yes it's a bad news because [you]
9	L:	[no but that's] good news=
10	T:	=that's good news G N good news …
11	L2:	ok so this one? (laughter)
12	LL:	/oh/ yes that's correct /yeah/ …
13	L1:	so=
14	LL:	/((3))/ he's sick/ he's/show me this one/=

15   L1:   =no! it's my card excuse me
16   T: so what's up you have to say the bad news=
17   L2:   =bad news because you can't ski=

Although we can see that the interaction is still organised around the activity the students are involved in, as evidenced by their 'on-task' comments, note how learners are given far more interactional space and manage the turn-taking themselves. The teacher is still involved, but only intervenes when necessary to clarify at lines 10 and 16. There is an absence of the IRF exchange structure found in extract 4.3, and, seemingly, far more freedom of topic choice. Closer analysis, however, reveals that this is in fact not the case; while learners certainly have more freedom to self-select or remain silent, contributions are made in response to the task. Although there is clear evidence of negotiation for meaning (Pica 1997; Long 1983, 1996) (in 2, 3, 5, 7, 8, 9) and learners contribute using their own words, they still orient the discourse to the pedagogic goals provided by the material.

In materials mode, then, patterns of interaction evolve from the material which determines turn-taking and topic choice; the interaction may or may not be managed exclusively by the teacher. Though learners have varying degrees of interactional space, depending on the nature of the activity, their contributions are still bounded by the constraints imposed by the task in hand.

4.2.3 Skills and systems mode

In skills and systems mode, pedagogic goals are closely related to providing language practice in relation to a particular language system (phonology, grammar, vocabulary, discourse) or language skill (reading, listening, writing, speaking). Teaching objectives may also relate to the development of specific learner strategies. Typically, the interaction in this mode follows a lockstep organisation and the IRF sequence frequently occurs. Turn-taking and topic selection are determined by the target language and responsibility for managing the turn-taking usually lies with the teacher. Pedagogic goals are oriented towards accuracy rather than fluency and the teacher's concern is to get learners to produce strings of accurate linguistic forms and manipulate the target language. Direct repair and scaffolding have an important role to play as illustrated in the next extract.

One of the main pedagogic goals of skills and systems mode is to get learners to manipulate target forms, illustrated in extract 4.5 in which the teacher uses cued drills to practise a particular form.

Extract 4.5
1   T: (writes on board) hmm lets practice this ok ah lets follow this pattern it was mmm
2   that he mmm ok eh for example if I say to you cold … froze … you have to say it was
3   SO cold that he froze but if I say to you cold DAY froze it was such a cold day that he
4   froze ok eh (16) exciting cry (5) exciting cry (2)
5   L2: it was so exciting that he he cried=
6   T: =it was so exciting that he CRIED yeah ok (3) exciting FOOTBALL match

```
 7        had a heart ATTACK =
 8  L:    =heart attack (laughter)
 9  L1:   it was such an exciting football match that I ((1))=
10  T:    =had a heart attack it was SUCH an exciting football match that I had a
11        heart attack eh (13) FAST train arrived in the morning (4) fast train arrived in one
12        hour (4) it was SUCH a fast train…
13  L2:   he ar ar arrived=
14  T:    =that he arrived … in one hour=
15  L2:   =in one hour=
16  T:    =ok lets change it to HE (writes on board) and lets make it RUDE man
17        went away Mikey…
18  L:    he was so rude he was such a rude=
19  T:    =such a rude?…
20  L:    man=
21  T:    =man …
22  L:    that I (2)
23  T:    went away…
24  L:    I went away=
```

Here, learners are prompted by the teacher's cues to produce accurate forms in lines 4 and 6. Little attention is paid to meaning and the teacher's pedagogic goal is to prompt, repair and display correct forms through echo (in 6 and 10). Scaffolding and direct repair occur again (14, 19) and the turn-taking and choice of topic are directed by the teacher who manages the interaction. Learners are afforded little interactional space – a deliberate strategy on the part of the teacher given her intention at this point in the lesson: to practise the structure *so … that* and *such … that* with past tense verb forms.

The type of teacher-initiated practice witnessed in this extract is typical of skills and systems mode. Unlike materials mode, where language practice evolves around a piece of material, in skills and systems mode, it evolves from teacher prompts and is managed by the teacher. Indeed, learner contributions typically go *through* the teacher for evaluation, confirmation or repair. This type of teaching is often referred to as *deductive*: it is heavily controlled by the teacher and well-suited to the kinds of language practice normally found in lower ability groups. At higher levels, on the other hand, there is more scope for *inductive* teaching, using discovery-based approaches to learning and allowing learners the opportunity to 'work things out' for themselves. Clearly, patterns of turn-taking in a skills and systems mode are strongly influenced by the extent to which the teacher's methodology is broadly inductive (where students work more independently) or deductive (where teachers maintain tight control of the interaction).

Extract 4.6, for example, in which an upper intermediate class is working on their writing skills, portrays a broadly inductive teaching-learning context.

Extract 4.6

```
1  T:    =yes so tell me again what you mean by that?=
2  L:    =the first is the introduction the second eh in this case we have the ((3))
```

3   who you are to eh introduce yourself a few words about yourself and
4   where you live and what I do [and]
5   T: [so]…yes?=
6   L: =and then it's the problem what happened …
7   T: yes=
8   L: =and you need to explain it and why you are writing because probably you did
9   something like you gave the information to the police but it didn't happen …
10   T: right=
11   L: =which is why it's ((2))=
12   T: =so can I ask you why did you write it in your head as you said?=
13   L: =I don't know it's like a rule=
14   T: =right so it's like a rule what do you mean? …
15   L: =like I don't think about this I [eh I]
16   T: [ok alright] did anybody else follow eh writing it in
17   your head kind of way? It seems to me it seems to me that this information here is is
18   quite clear I it's clearly laid down it's not like asking and eh writing an essay about
19   nuclear [deterrents]

In this extract, there is evidence of more equal patterns of turn-taking; indeed, learner turns are, at times, significantly longer than the teacher's (lines 2–4, 8–9). Throughout, the teacher adopts a less evaluative role and instead seeks to clarify (1, 5, 12, 14) and elicit descriptions of the learners' writing strategies. Clarification requests are extremely valuable in promoting opportunities for learning since they 'compel' learners to reformulate their contribution, by rephrasing or paraphrasing. There is clear evidence in this extract that the teacher's unwillingness to accept the learner's first contribution (in 5, 14) promotes a longer turn and a more elaborated response. This process of allowing learners to struggle and then helping them to produce longer, fuller, more elaborate responses is central to dialogic teaching (Mercer 2009). Although certain types of *task* often result in modified interaction, it is the teacher who is arguably better placed to seek clarification and get a reformulated response, as demonstrated in extract 4.6.

It is interesting to note that although the two extracts above are examples of skills and systems mode, their interactional features are quite different. Extract 4.6 is characterised by extended learner turns as the teacher, through prompts and referential questions, seeks to clarify a learner's contribution. Interactional space is provided to allow the learner an opportunity to explain her writing strategies. In 4.5, on the other hand, extended teacher turns are the main feature of this IRF sequence. Learners respond to cues, attending to form and adjusting their response in line with the corrective feedback they receive. Thus, although the patterns of turn-taking and relative quantities of teacher and learner talk are *different*, both extracts are examples of the same mode because the pedagogic focus is related to language skills and systems.

To summarise, in skills and systems mode, the focus is a specific language system or sub-skill. Learning outcomes are typically achieved through tightly controlled turn-taking and topic selection, determined by the teacher. Learners respond to teacher prompts in an endeavour to produce linguistically accurate strings of utterances. The interaction is typically (though not exclusively) form-focused, characterised by extended teacher turns, display questions and direct repair.

4.2.4 Classroom context mode

In classroom context mode, there is a shift from teacher-directed interaction to discourse which is more symmetrical, with teacher and learners playing a more equal role. Opportunities for genuine communication are frequent and the teacher plays a less prominent role, taking more of a 'back seat' and allowing learners all the interactional space they need. The principal role of the teacher is to listen and support the interaction, which frequently takes on the appearance of a naturally occurring conversation. Classroom context mode is frequently found in situations where the teacher is eliciting opinions or ideas or giving students an opportunity to discuss their experiences. The principal interactional features to be found include extended learner turns (learners manage both who speaks and when, and direct the topic); correspondingly shorter teacher turns; the use of direct repair to quickly fix interactional trouble; feedback on the message rather than language forms, content feedback; wide use of referential or genuine questions; scaffolding to help learners express their ideas; requests for clarification and confirmation checks.

Extract 4.7 below is taken from a class with a group of advanced, multilingual learners. The teacher's stated aim is 'to generate discussion prior to a cloze exercise on poltergeists' and learners have been invited to share their experiences.

Extract 4.7

```
256   L3:   =ahh nah the one thing that happens when a person dies ((2)) my mother
257         used to work with old people and when they died … the last thing that went
258         out was the hearing ((4)) about this person =
259   T:    =aha (2)
260   L3:   so I mean even if you are unconscious or on drugs or something I mean
261         it's probably still perhaps can hear what's happened (2)
262   L2:   but it gets ((2))=
263   LL:   /but it gets/there are ((2))/=
264   L3:   =I mean you have seen so many operation ((3)) and so you can imagine
265         and when you are hearing the sounds of what happens I think you can get a
266         pretty clear picture of what's really going on there=
267   L:    =yeah=
268   L:    =and and …
269   L1:   but eh and eh I don't know about other people but eh ((6)) I always have
270         feeling somebody watching watch watches me=
271   T:    =yes=
272   L4:   =YEAH=
273   L1:   =somebody just follow me either a man or a woman I don't know if it's a
274         man I feel really exciting if it's a woman ((4)) I don't know why like I'm
275         trying to
276         do things better like I'm eh … look like this … you FEEL it … I don't know=
277   T:    =you think it's a kind of spirit =
278   L1:   =I think it's just yeah somebody who lives inside us and ((3))… visible area …
```

```
279   L4:   I would say it's just neurotic problems (laughter)
280   L1:   what what …
281   L4:   nothing nothing nothing…
282   L1:   but have you seen city of angels=
283   L4:   =no I haven't =
284   L1:   =with eh Meg Ryan and eh Nicholas Cage it's a wonderful story and I think
285         it's true actually=
286   T:    =and does this bother you =
287   L1:   =what?=
288   T:    =this feeling that you get does it bother you?=
289   L1:   =it's eh you know when I am alone I'm ok but if I feel that somebody is
290         near I would be nervous=
291   T:    =I would be very nervous …
```

The most noticeable feature of the discourse in this extract is that the turn-taking is almost entirely managed by the learners, with evidence of competition for the floor and turn gaining, holding and passing. Turns are also significantly longer, contain more overlaps and latches, and pausing is more pronounced. In 261 for example, the 2-second pause at the end of learner 3's turn is perceived by other learners as an invitation to take up the discussion and two learners take a turn in 262 and 263, before the original speaker (L3) regains the floor in 264. Topic shifts are also managed by the learners (in 264, 269, 282), with the teacher responding more as an equal participant, allowing the discourse to develop within the topic frames selected by the learners. Note how in 281 the sub-topic of 'neuroses' is not developed and the original speaker retakes the floor in 282, shifting to a new topic. The only questions asked by the teacher are referential (in 277, 286, 288) and extended learner turns dominate the sequence. Errors go unrepaired, there are no evaluative comments and the only feedback given is content-based, normally in the shape of a personal reaction.

The predominant interactional feature of extract 4.7 is the local management of the speech exchange system; learners have considerable freedom as to what to say and when. This process of 'topicalisation' (Slimani 1989), where learners select and develop a topic, is significant in maximising learning potential since 'whatever is topicalised by the learners rather than the teacher has a better chance of being claimed to have been learnt' (Ellis 1998: 159). In this extract, the academic task structure and social participation structure (Johnson, 1995) are clearly more relaxed and opportunities for learning are increased. In many classroom contexts, however, it is not uncommon for teachers to retain control of the interaction, interrupting students and taking control of the topic. While this may be inevitable, there are times, as in classroom context mode, when relinquishing control of turn-taking and topic choice are fundamental interactional strategies. This is, arguably, a skill which more teachers need to develop if more even, equal participation structures are to be achieved.

The defining characteristic of classroom context mode, then, is interactional space: extended learner turns predominate as participants co-construct the discourse. Teacher feedback shifts its focus from form to content, and error correction is minimal. In short, the orientation is towards maintaining genuine communication rather than displaying linguistic knowledge.

TASK 4.2

In the following extract, identify the modes which are in operation. Where does one mode end and another begin? How does the teacher move from one mode to another? How successful is she in achieving her pedagogic goals?

Extract 4.8

(In the extract, a group of intermediate level adult learners are preparing to read a text called 'Pot Luck Suppers'. Leslie is a character in the course-book and Yvette, Georgia and Haldoun are all students in the class. The teacher's pedagogic goal is to establish a context prior to reading.)

29 T: =yes olive oil yes yes must be a good quality=
30 L: =and the other olive oil vegetable and made from maize from corn=
31 T: =yes corn oil and yeah there's many different types of oil olive oil is the bes
32   and … essential to Spanish omelette tortilla erm right so if you were invited to
33   one of Leslie's pot-luck suppers (referring to the book) erm right what would
34   you bring … along … with you?
35 L: American or ((1))?
36 T: yes this is this Leslie the American woman imagine she [invited you to a pot
37   luck supper
38 L: [a bottle of wine
39 T: a bottle of wine yes
40 L: a dish   [of food
41 T: [what else? a dish of food yes what=
42 L: =dessert
43 T: yes possibly a dessert=
44 L: =or a starter
45 T: or a starter (.) yes so how would you know what to bring?
46 LL: ((2)) the organiser give you a list ((1))
47 T: that's right yes so it's it's quite well-organised you can (laughs) imagine
48   writing a list oh yes I'll ask Yvette she can bring a starter (.) oh Georgia a nice
49   salad Italians are very good with salads and then maybe a main course er
50   Haldoun and perhaps er the Japanese can do some more some more main
51   courses so it would be very er very well-organised=
52 L: =usually ((2)) like sometimes there are like 3 main courses ((2)) like
53   graduation in sometimes we have parties and we have like er roast chicken
54   and another people
55   bring ((3)) for the main courses and we don't have nothing for nothing for
56   dessert and nothing for the starter [(laughs)]
57 T: [(laughs)] oh dear well Georgia perhaps
58   when you go back to Italy perhaps you can organise one of these typical pot-
59   luck suppers and organise it well so you'll have plenty of desserts and plenty
60   of starters (laughs) but er do you think it's a good idea?
61 L: sometimes, yeah

62	L:	it's nice because you don't know what you're going to eat=
63	T:	=it's a surprise yes, yeah as long as you like everything … I mean some
64		people don't like certain things what adjective do we use for people who don't
65		like that and hate that and a lot of food they won't eat … we call it people are
66		very … FUSsy fussy with their food (**writes on BB**) right so fussy that's don't
67		like vegetables, never eat er pasta (laughs)=
68	L1:	= excuse me how to say if er you ((2)) for example if you try some burger on
69		corner …on the the street and then you feel not very well
70	T:	er … I'm not quite sure what you mean Yvette if you?
71	L1:	you can buy for example ((2)) just on the street
72	T:	you mean street sellers … people selling food on the street yes

So far, the discussion has focused on the importance of recognising that all classroom discourse is made up of a series of micro-contexts, called modes, each with distinctive pedagogic goals and specific interactional features. We now look in more detail at the various interactional features, which I call *interactures*.

Table 4.2 presents a summary of the thirteen interactures used in the SETT framework.

Table 4.2   *SETT Interactures*

Interacture	Description
A. Scaffolding	1. Reformulation (rephrasing a learner's contribution). 2. Extension (extending a learner's contribution). 3. Modelling (providing an example for learner(s)).
B. Direct repair	Correcting an error quickly and directly.
C. Content feedback	Giving feedback to the message rather than the words used.
D. Extended wait-time	Allowing sufficient time (several seconds) for students to respond or formulate a response.
E. Referential question	Genuine questions to which the teacher does not know the answer.
F. Seeking clarification	1. Teacher asks a student to clarify something the student has said. 2. Student asks teacher to clarify something the teacher has said.
G. Extended learner turn	Learner turn of more than one utterance.
H. Teacher echo	1. Teacher repeats teacher's previous utterance. 2. Teacher repeats a learner's contribution.
I. Teacher interruptions	Interrupting a learner's contribution.
J. Extended teacher turn	Teacher turn of more than one utterance.
K. Turn completion	Completing a learner's contribution for the learner.
L. Display question	Asking questions to which teacher knows the answer.
M. Form-focused feedback	Giving feedback on the words used, not the message.

The interactures used in the SETT framework can be found in varying degrees in any classroom. They are intended to be representative rather than exhaustive, and do not claim to account for all types of verbal behaviour. The reader is reminded, for example, that the focus is on teachers' use of language so there are no interactures specifically for describing learner interaction, though, in fact, learners do use some of the interactional features listed here. The extent to which a particular interacture is used is dependent on the context and teacher's agenda at a point in time. Some are more common than others and occur with greater regularity throughout the discourse; display questions, for example, are more widespread than referential, or genuine, questions. Display questions are also more widespread among lower levels. It is also very important to note that certain interactures are more *appropriate* to a particular mode: clarification requests, for example, are typically found in classroom context mode, whereas teacher interruptions may be found in skills and systems mode. An interacture, then, can be defined as a particular interactional feature which 'belongs to' or is typical of a specific mode. An interacture can be regarded as being more or less appropriate, or *mode convergent*, at a given moment in a lesson according to a teacher's desired learning outcomes. By studying their use of interactures, teachers can very quickly establish a profile of their verbal behaviour while teaching and make judgements concerning how appropriate or effective their use of language is in relation to desired pedagogic goals. Teachers who have used the SETT framework typically identify specific features which are not appropriate and make changes to their use of language based on these self-observations. What follows is a discussion of their observations and reflections.

In the extracts which follow, there is clear evidence that interactures are interpreted by teachers as being more or less 'relevant', 'appropriate' or 'necessary' according to mode, as an examination of extract 4.9, for example, reveals. Here, the teacher observes that given that the focus of her teaching was fluency rather than accuracy, turn completion, direct repair and form-focused feedback 'didn't fit in'. She also makes the point that learner needs are a strong determinant of the kind of interactures which should be adopted, providing further evidence of the need to use language which is both appropriate to pedagogic goals and learner needs at a particular moment.

Extract 4.9
I didn't do any completing of turns, form-focused feedback didn't fit in really and there was no direct repair really because I suppose it was fluency rather than accuracy and I didn't give anybody any extended wait-time because I didn't think it was necessary but I would have done it if they had needed it.

Judgements concerning the relevance or appropriacy of a particular interacture are made retrospectively in the light of desired teaching/learning outcomes or in reaction to learner needs. It is not the suggestion that such decisions are taken consciously 'in the heat' of a teaching moment, merely that they can be usefully studied as part of the reflective process of SETT.

In addition to demonstrating an awareness of the appropriacy of interactures according to mode, mention was also made on more than one occasion of the 'dangers' of transferring interactures which are appropriate in one context to another where they are less appropriate. In extract 4.10, for example, there is a recognition by the teacher that the interactures she identified as being appropriate may well be transferred to a mode where they are less appropriate or *mode divergent*.

Extract 4.10
It will be interesting to see whether the features that I identified most clearly were that, a mixture of reformulation and direct repair, extended wait-time, echo, form-focused feedback, turn completion. Now I think I think in the context that was fairly appropriate but I think I would be inclined to do that when it's NOT necessary and I'd be interested to see if that's a feature of a different kind of lesson.

In this extract, there is a sense that while certain interactures may well be more appropriate in one mode than another, teachers' habits, particular features of their language use, may prevent appropriate verbal behaviour: 'I think I would be inclined to do that when it's NOT necessary'. Clearly, a large part of using SETT is concerned to alert teachers to features of their own teacher talk and compare those features with interactures which are mode convergent.

4.3 SETT AND TEACHER DEVELOPMENT

From the discussion so far, the reader may be under the impression that L2 classroom interaction can be classified very neatly into a finite number of modes, each with its own particular set of pedagogic and interactional features. This is clearly not the case. As mentioned before, the SETT framework is a generic instrument which is intended to be *representative* rather than comprehensive. It was always intended that it should be modified to suit a particular context and that teachers should adapt it to suit their own particular needs. While the four modes are clearly delineated by pedagogic goals and interactional features, they cannot account for every single aspect of classroom discourse, nor are they able to describe all features in every context. The first difficulty in using SETT is that it is incapable of describing all aspects of classroom interaction. For example, interactions which are not teacher-fronted, where learners work independently of the teacher, are not described, though there is no reason why it could not be adapted for this purpose. Rather, the framework is concerned to establish an understanding of the relationship between interaction and learning; specifically, the interface between teaching objectives and teacher talk. In essence, as a tool for teacher development it has to enable teachers to describe interaction relatively easily and unambiguously. Yet tensions are inevitable.

In the discussion which follows, I consider how SETT might be used as a tool for reflective practice and as part of a teacher development process. Essentially, we are interested in the extent to which SETT is able to cope with the rapid, fast-changing, multi-layered interactions which make up L2 classroom discourse. The 'neat and tidy' examples presented in the earlier part of this chapter can be found, but more often than not modes occur in combination with other modes, rather than in isolation. Interactional decisions are taken in the 'here and now' of a lesson, the moment by moment sequence of planning and action, influenced by many factors, including time constraints, teacher and learner agendas, the interdependence of turns, unexpected occurrences. Lessons rarely progress from A to Z; as in conversations, deviations, topic-shifts, back-channelling, repetitions, false-starts and overlaps all occur very regularly, making description difficult to achieve.

Movement between modes, henceforth *mode-switching*, is a very common phenomenon, instigated either by teachers or learners, though normally by teachers as they manage the interaction. The result is the same: the interaction becomes multi-layered and more difficult to interpret and describe. In theory, any participant in the discourse can say anything at any time and the ensuing interaction takes sudden twists and turns in direction, which make analysis difficult. In practice, this rarely occurs owing to the fact that classroom interaction is goal-oriented. Understanding is gained by considering the inter-relatedness of the turn-taking, the fact that turns do not occur in isolation, and by identifying pedagogic goals.

It is important to note here that mode switches occur very rapidly and over a short space of time. In order to 'find their way' in the discourse, learners have to be alert to these extremely rapid switches and learn to 'read the signals' so that interaction is maintained (see Breen 1998); there are many instances in the data where such rapid and often unmarked mode-switching does result in communication breakdown which may or may not be repaired.

Indeed, it might be argued that one of the hallmarks of effective teaching is a teacher's ability to switch from one mode to another while keeping the class together. From a teacher development perspective, it would be quite useful for teachers, using SETT, to note the ways in which they move from one stage of a lesson to another and to note the extent to which language use and pedagogic goals do or do not converge. Noticing how specific discourse markers are used to manage transitions, or focusing on particular interactures which indicate the beginning or end of a mode, are also useful ways of raising awareness and improving classroom interactional competence.

In addition to mode switching, a commonly found type of mixed mode occurs when there is a brief departure from a main to a secondary mode and back to the main mode again. For example, the pattern may be classroom-context-skills-and-systems-classroom-context, with classroom context the main mode and skills and systems the secondary mode. Sequences like this are henceforth referred to as *mode side sequences*. Side sequences are a common feature of conversation and involve two speakers jointly constructing and negotiating the dialogue, 'feeling their way forward together' (Cook 1989: 54) and managing two topics and two exchange structures. Equally, in the L2 classroom, participants progress tentatively, each pursuing a particular agenda which is typically related to that of the institution. Mode side sequences occur quite frequently, as exemplified in extract 4.11, in which a group of a advanced learners is discussing life after death.

Extract 4.11

109	T:	[no ok alright] … so Jan you want to live forever?=
110	L3:	=yeah if money can afford it I will freeze body=
111	L:	=ugh…
112	L1:	what are you going to do? … frozen frozen you body?=
113	L3:	=yeah=
114	L1:	cyonics?…
115	T:	=yeah it's cry cry cryo[genics]
116	L1:	[cryonics] cryogenics … no cryonics=
117	T:	=oh is it? ok=
118	L1:	=I think so I don't know …
11	T:	let me check it it might be in this one …(looks in dictionary)
120	L:	((4))…
121	T:	cryogenics if you don't freeze your body you freeze your head isn't that the
122		way it is?=
123	L:	=you can choose=
124	T:	=oh really?=
125	L3:	=it's eh a ((2))…
126	T:	I see so if you don't believe in religion=
127	L:	=yeah=

The main mode is classroom context, with a focus on personal experiences. The mode side sequence occurs at lines 114 to 124, with L1's question 'cyonics?' which switches to the secondary mode, skills and systems. This language-related question prompts a brief discussion in which the teacher checks the vocabulary item in a dictionary. Once the vocabulary question has been cleared up, the teacher brings the discussion back to classroom context mode at line 126. The impetus for a mode side sequence may come from either a learner or the teacher, but it is very often the teacher who brings the discussion 'back on track', returning to the original mode. Here, there is evidence of a departure to skills and systems mode in order to clarify a language-related matter, but the departure is relatively brief and the main mode is quickly re-established.

From a teacher development perspective, it would be useful for teachers to identify mode side sequences and study the ways in which they are managed. In my own experience, teachers frequently switch momentarily to a secondary mode, but do not always switch back to the main mode. This is especially true of a move from classroom context to skills and systems; the language focus may quickly take over any prior class discussion with the teacher resuming a more authoritative position and any opportunities for learner interaction becoming lost. Using SETT allows teachers to observe their ability to manage both side sequences and switches, both of which are important to classroom interactional competence.

In brief, then, we can say that mode side sequences occur when there is a momentary shift from one (main) mode to another (secondary) mode in response to a change in pedagogic goals. A number of such mode side sequences have been identified, each following a similar pattern:

- classroom-context–skills-and-systems–classroom-context
- materials–skills-and-systems–materials
- materials–classroom-context–materials
- managerial–skills-and-systems–managerial

Both teacher and learners initiate mode side sequences, but the responsibility for returning to the main mode lies with the teacher. The extent to which the teacher is able to 'keep on track' and ensure that learners do not become 'lost' is closely related to teachers' ability to move from one mode to another, adjusting language to the unfolding text of the lesson. A mode side sequence is symbolised by an immediate and obvious change in the talk-in-interaction, with different interactional features and a different speech exchange system.

TASK 4.3
Make a 10–15 minute recording of one of your classes, or, alternatively, watch a video clip of someone else teaching. Analyse the discourse using SETT and identify which modes are used and which interactures can be identified. (You may want to use Tables 4.1 and 4.2 to help you.) Note any examples of mode switching or mode side sequence. Evaluate the teaching in terms of its potential to promote learning; which features of CIC did you identify?

4.4 SUMMARY

The descriptive framework presented in this chapter is designed to enable teachers to develop a closer understanding of the interactional organisation of their classes. The SETT framework is intended as a means to an end rather than the end itself, concerned to facilitate understanding, rather than code every interaction. Consequently, it is representative, not comprehensive. Given the uniqueness of the L2 classroom and the fact that every interaction is locally produced, it is neither practicable nor realistic to propose that an all-encompassing view of context can be derived, or that an instrument is available which can accurately provide an emic perspective of each interaction. The framework is intended to be both generic and yet adaptable to suit a particular context.

SETT promotes an understanding of the relationship between pedagogic purpose and language use, enabling teachers to identify 'recurrent segmental patterns or structures' (Drew 1994: 142) which can contribute to an understanding of what constitutes appropriate teacher talk in a particular mode. This dynamic perspective is intended to avoid the need for bland descriptive systems which adopt an invariant view of L2 classroom interaction. By getting teachers to relate their use of language to pedagogic goals and by examining interactional features in each of the four modes, it is anticipated that a greater depth of understanding can be gained in a relatively short space of time.

In the data, four modes were identified and described according to their pedagogic goals and interactional features. Each mode has its own characteristic fingerprint (Heritage and Greatbach 1991), specific interactional features which are related to teaching objectives. While the characteristics identified in each mode have a certain uniformity, there is also some degree of heterogeneity (Seedhouse 1996) determined by the precise nature of the local context and including factors such as the level of the students and the methodology being used.

Modes are not static and invariant, but dynamic and changing. There are movements from one mode to another (*mode switching*) and between main and secondary modes (*mode side sequences*). Although learners may initiate a switch, the responsibility for returning to the main mode typically lies with the teacher. Switches from one mode to another are marked by *transition* or *boundary* markers (*right, now, ok*, etc.) with a corresponding adjustment in intonation and sentence stress. A mode may last for one whole lesson or for much shorter periods, with more frequent changes.

Teachers may use the SETT grid as a means of understanding the extent to which their verbal behaviour is *mode convergent*, where pedagogic goals and language use are congruent, or *mode divergent*, where inconsistencies in pedagogic goals and interactional features hinder opportunities for learning. In addition, SETT can be used as a way of developing closer understandings of classroom interaction in a move towards classroom interactional competence (see Chapter 3).

Chapter 5

Researching classroom discourse

Throughout this book, I have made the case for teachers, as active reflective practitioners, to become researchers of their classroom practices. There are essentially three elements to this argument, discussed in previous chapters and summarised here. First, in order to develop, teachers need to first understand their own *context*. Like other researchers (see, for example, Bax 2003; Kumaravadivelu 1999; Wallace 1998), I have argued that teacher-researchers, as both producers and consumers of their research, should be concerned to enhance understanding of their local context rather than generalise to a broader one. Such an understanding entails a fine-grained, up-close study of local practices, rather than the kind of broad-brush approaches which are often adopted. Developing understandings of local context lies at the heart of this book and is central to both professional development and effective teaching and learning.

Second, any understanding of context entails first describing and then developing an awareness of professional practice. Both should be based on evidence as argued in Chapter 1. Although there are many ways of collecting and analysing evidence, I have suggested that the best way to make evidence-based decisions is to collect *data*. The logical conclusion of this aspect of my argument is that teachers' ability to collect and analyse data is central to their professional development. In this chapter, we'll be considering in more detail how teacher-researchers might go about the process of data collection and analysis.

The third element of the argument is that *interaction* lies at the heart of all effective classroom practice and that teachers should therefore focus at least some of their attention on an understanding of interactional processes. In Chapter 3, I introduced the notion of classroom interactional competence, defined as 'a teacher's ability to use language and interaction as a means of mediating learning'. In Chapter 4, we looked at one approach to enhancing classroom interactional competence using the SETT framework. In this chapter, we'll be considering alternative ways of both collecting data and studying classroom interaction.

According to Kumaravadivelu any attempt to understand classrooms must begin with description:

> What actually happens there [in the classroom] largely determines the degree to which desired learning outcomes are realized. The task of systematically observing,

analysing and understanding classroom aims and events therefore becomes central to any serious educational enterprise. (Kumaravadivelu 1999: 454)

Essentially, the point being made here is that teachers have a responsibility to accurately describe their classroom practices in order to ensure that their pedagogic goals are achieved. In order to fully understand those practices, I propose, teachers need to be able to select and master specific tools – it is these tools which are presented here. In the sections which follow, a critique is presented of some of the principal approaches which could be used to collect data and make evidence-based decisions. A critique is offered of corpus-based approaches to data collection and analysis, including corpus linguistics and a combined conversation analysis/corpus linguistics methodology.

Collecting classroom data nearly always entails making a recording and may require some kind of transcription, either full or partial. In the first section of this chapter, I address the issues involved in recording and transcribing classroom data, including ethical considerations.

5.1 RECORDING, TRANSCRIPTION AND ETHICS

(For a full account of the issues and difficulties associated with transcription, the reader is referred to Jenks 2011.)

TASK 5.1
What difficulties do you think you would encounter in making a recording (audio or video) of a second language classroom? How might you deal with some of those difficulties?

In any second language classroom, there is far too much happening at any one time to capture every interaction, every word, every gesture. Multiple interactions are the norm and multi-party talk underpins every action, every activity, every moment. Not only are there technical problems associated with *recording* what actually happens, there are, more importantly, enormous issues associated with *representing* spoken discourse as written text. Making a recording, in itself, is highly complex and fraught with difficulty. While making an audio recording is, in many ways, the easiest means of capturing spoken interaction in classrooms, there is always the issue of background noise or interference. This can become a real problem during playback and make key moments in a lesson impossible to decipher. Solutions include the use of digital recorders positioned carefully around the room, or the use of lapel microphones or multi-directional microphones which are more sensitive and may result in higher quality recordings. Essentially, the more devices that are used, the better will be the chance of making a decent recording.

Video recordings are a relatively straightforward means of recording interaction in the classroom and have the added advantage of providing a visual representation of what happened. Many of the unspoken gestures and paralanguage to be found in classrooms communicate as much (if not more) than the spoken words. To get the best recordings, it is normally preferred to use two cameras: one at the front of the classroom pointing to the back, one at the back pointing to the front. In this way, it is possible to record all the interaction taking place, especially if video cameras are supplemented by the use of digital recorders positioned around the room. This system normally means that it is possible to capture all actions and spoken interactions. The main disadvantage with the use of video is that it can be quite intrusive and result in unusual or unexpected behaviour by students or teachers. The other issue is how to transcribe gestures, body movements, actions, etc., in the written representation of a lesson.

A third possibility is the use of observation, either self- or peer-observation. The main difficulty in using observers is that they usually have to be trained in the use of an observation schedule (see 'interaction analysis' below), and may not be able to record every detail of the interaction. Owing to the complexity of classroom interaction, it is unlikely that two observers would record what they saw in exactly the same way; there are then issues around the reliability of the data and the extent to which the observation is a faithful record of the class. One way of making observation more objective is to use 'focused observation', whereby the observer focuses on one detail in the interaction such as teacher's use of questions, oral feedback, learner involvement, etc. This approach has the advantage of allowing the observer to focus on only one element in the interaction and ignore everything else. Self-observation requires the use of some kind of recording and possibly an instrument such as SETT (see Chapter 4); the main advantage is that it is quick and easy to organise, but may lack objectivity.

There are a range of principles which should be followed when making a recording. First, ethical issues must be taken into consideration. Written and signed permission must be obtained from all participants before any recording can begin, and in the case of young children, this may also involve getting the permission of parents. In some contexts, the faces of students must not be visible in order to protect their identity. Participants must be told what the recording will be used for, how it will be used and how their anonymity will be ensured. They must have the option of being able to opt in or out of the recording and to leave at any time (see BERA guidelines on research ethics: http://www.bera.ac.uk).

A key question which many teachers ask when making a recording is 'how much data do I need?' The amount of data collected will depend both on the purpose of the recording and the approach to analysis. For example, a very detailed transcript of one lesson may be sufficient for investigating one issue; alternatively, a few recordings across a range of lessons may be preferred if there is little or no transcription. Most teacher-researchers find they have too much data and are unable to make adequate use of it, so this is an issue which is worth careful consideration.

The quality of the recording will greatly influence the use to which it can be put. For audio and video recordings, steps need to be taken to ensure that the best quality recordings are made. There is nothing more frustrating than working with recordings where only part of the interaction can be heard. Things to think about include: the choice of room, the use of carpet and curtains to help reduce 'echo', positioning of equipment, number of recorders, selective recording where only some of the participants are included, and so on.

If you decide to collect data by observation, consideration should be given to the precise role of the observer and their position and involvement in the lesson. In cases where the observer is also another teacher, how might this affect the group dynamics? Where should the observer sit and what part should they play in the lesson? What is the potential for bias, or lack of objectivity? In addition, it might be best to 'set the agenda' before the observation begins: agreeing what the focus is can save a huge amount of time and minimise disagreements later on. A focused observation is also more likely to be productive.

Once a recording has been made, you may or may not wish to transcribe it, either in full or partially. The main concern of transcription is to 'represent reality' as accurately and faithfully as possible. There has been much discussion and debate on this over past decades and there is still only partial agreement as to the extent to which a written transcript can accurately re-present a spoken encounter. Essentially, it is impossible to capture in writing what has been said – even the most detailed transcripts cannot achieve this. But there are extremes of detail: a transcript may offer a rather bland summary of an encounter or a highly detailed description which attempts to record every detail. Decisions must be taken at the outset concerning levels of detail: do we opt for broad or narrow transcripts, for example? A broad transcript captures the essence of what was said, the words themselves or even their intended meaning, but ignores the fine details such as a stressed syllable, a pause, a rising intonation, overlapping speech. These technical difficulties remain as much of a problem for transcribers as they have always done.

Perhaps more importantly, there are factors to consider which go beyond the purely technical side of transcription. Methodological decisions made at the time a transcript is produced will greatly influence our understandings of a particular discourse encounter such as a second language class. The precise relationship between the interaction which took place and the words and symbols used to represent it is crucial and complex. That relationship involves the transcriber making key decisions such as:

- Do I include all pauses and how do I represent them?
- How do I record particular gestures, facial expressions, body movements, etc. – or do I simply ignore them?
- What is the 'correct' way to record emphatic speech? Do I even need to record it?
- Do I organise the written text by turn at talk, as conversation analysts do, or by linguistic utterance, showing breath groups and intonation?
- Should intonation be included – if so how do I record it?
- Do I need to transcribe everything – or even anything? (Walsh 2011)

Bucholz (2007) offers a very poignant example of the need for transcription to be done well and include an appropriate level of detail. She takes two transcripts of the same event and demonstrates how each offers a different interpretation of that event. Both transcripts relate to a research project on nerdy American teenagers, conducted in 1998. Each transcript offers a written account of an interview which the author conducted with one teenager.

Extract 5.1

> Fred: We're always the nerds. We like it. We're glad to be the nerds and the squares. We don't drink, we don't do any drugs, we just get naturally high, we do insane funny things. And we're smart. We get good grades.

In this first extract, the main details of the original interview have been retained. As we read the extract, we get a good sense of Fred's feelings of being a nerd, what this means, why they like it and so on. From an interviewer's perspective, it seems to offer sufficient detail of the interview, without burdening the reader with 'unnecessary' detail. Essentially, extract 5.1 is a summary of the interview and is highly typical of the kind of data used as 'evidence' in qualitative research reporting interviews. While it certainly captures the essence of that encounter, it omits all the detail of the inter-action.

In contrast, consider extract 5.2 below, which offers a micro-analytic rendition of the same event. Here, it is interesting to note how the two speakers jointly created meaning and the ways in which the interviewer (Mary) actually did quite a lot of work to elicit Fred's intended meaning.

Extract 5.2

1	Mary:	[So]
2	Fred:	[We're al]ways the nerds.
3		We like it.
4	Mary:	You@'re the nerds?
5	Fred:	We're <creaky> {glad} to be the ner:ds,
6		a@nd the squa:res and,
7	Mary:	Is that what
8	Fred:	[we don't–]
9	Mary:	[you say] you are?
10	Fred:	<[i□]> Well,
11		we don't exactly s:–
12		We don't always say it,=
13		=I say it. n@
14	Mary:	@@[@!]
15	Fred:	[But–]
16	Mary:	@ You're [[prou:d.]]
17	Fred:	[[you]] know,
18	Mary:	[@@]

19	Fred:	[we don't–]
20		We just don't (0.5) drink,
21		we d [on't (.) <rapid> {d]o
22	Mary:	[Mm.]
23	Fred:	any drugs,}
24		we don't–
25		we just,
26		<smiling voice quality> {get ↑naturally high},
27	Mary:	A[ha:.]
28	Fred:	[@:]
29	Mary:	[[So that makes you nerds?]]
30	Fred:	[[We just do insane]] funny things.=
31		=I don't know,
32		maybe.
33		(0.6)
34	Mary:	So:=
35	Fred:	=And we're smart.
36		We get <[e□]>-
37		good grades.
38	(1.3) Mostly.

The details of this transcript reveal particular features which indicate that this interaction was a joint enterprise and that meanings were established together. There are a number of overlaps (in lines 1–2, 8–9, 16–17, etc., indicated [ ]), which normally suggest that both speakers are trying to establish mutual understanding; the use of acknowledgement tokens or backchannels (in lines 22 and 27) which demonstrate understanding by Mary; evidence of pausing (in lines 20, 33 and 38), which may indicate interactional trouble or pausing for thought; the use of latched turns (marked = in lines 12–13, 30–31, 34–35), indicating rapid speech or interruptions.

The overall impression we get as readers when we read extract 5.2 is that, rather than being boastful and triumphant, Fred is 'feeling her way' in the discourse, expressing herself with some difficulty and perhaps embarrassment. Mary, by contrast, prompts, guides and helps the interlocutor to say what she really mans, the hallmark of a good interviewer. As Bucholtz herself says:

> It is obvious that my original transcript was not merely woefully inadequate, but dangerously inaccurate in its representation of the interaction. Fred's comments are not the product of an autonomous, triumphant voice of nerd pride but are rather the result of considerable co-construction (and obstruction) by me as the researcher. (2007: 788)

This example highlights some of the dangers of summarising in a transcript the actual words used and demonstrates the need to try and capture and re-present the interaction as faithfully and as accurately as possible. Of course, the alternative is to avoid transcription completely by using some kind of instrument or frameworks (see Chapter 4).

In the next section, I provide a summary of three of the main approaches to researching classroom discourse: interaction analysis, discourse analysis and conversation analysis.

5.2 INTERACTION ANALYSIS, DISCOURSE ANALYSIS, CONVERSATION ANALYSIS

5.2.1 Interaction analysis

Interaction analysis entails the use of observation instruments, or *coding systems*, to record what an observer sees or thinks is happening at any given moment. According to Brown and Rodgers (2002), over 200 different observation instruments now exist, while Chaudron (1988) calculated that there were approximately twenty-six systems available for analysing interaction in the L2 classroom. Observation schedules use some system of recording such as ticking boxes, making marks and so on, usually at specific time intervals. They are often seen as being reliable, offering a more 'objective' record and allowing comparisons to be made. Following Wallace (1998), in the brief summary which follows, observation instruments are divided according to whether they are *system-based* or *ad hoc*.

By 'system' is meant that the instrument has a number of fixed categories which have been pre-determined by extensive trialling in different classroom contexts. There are several advantages to using a fixed system: the system is ready-made – there is no need to design one from scratch; because the system is well-known, there is no need for validation; any system may be used in real-time or following a recording; comparisons between one system and another are possible. One example of a system-based approach is that proposed by Flanders (1970), whose FIAC system (Flanders Interaction Analysis Categories) assigned classroom interaction to various categories of teacher and student talk:

Teacher talk
1. Accepts feelings
2. Praises or encourages
3. Accepts or uses ideas of pupils
4. Asks questions
5. Lectures
6. Gives direction
7. Criticises or uses authority

Pupil talk
8. Pupil talk: response
9. Pupil talk: initiation

Silence
10. Period of silence or confusion

Although this instrument has been widely used and, in one sense, has the potential to capture everything which might occur in a classroom, the categories are still rather broad and it is questionable whether the instrument could adequately account for the complex interactional organisation of the contemporary classroom. More recent observation schedules, such as COLT (Communicative Orientation to language Teaching, Allen et al. 1984), are more sophisticated and make use of a considerable range of both qualitative and quantitative modes of analysis. Nonetheless, system-based approaches to the study of classroom interaction are largely limited by their inability to adequately describe in detail what is happening in a local context. There are difficulties associated with matching patterns of interaction to the categories provided so that no allowance is made for events or interactions which do not 'fit' the categories. Observers may disagree over what they actually 'see' and no account is taken of the genuine complexity of classroom interaction.

In contrast to system-based interaction analysis, *ad hoc* approaches offer the construction of a more flexible instrument, which may, for example, be based on a specific classroom problem or area of interest. The instrument may be designed as part of an action research project in which practitioners wish to answer a particular question such as: how can I improve the quality of the feedback I give my students? Alternatively, the instrument might be designed through consultation with either teachers or students working in a specific context.

An example of an *ad hoc* approach to the study of classroom discourse was presented in Chapter 4; the SETT framework was designed in a specific context to investigate teachers' use of language. The main advantage is that it allows us, as observers, to focus on specific details in the interaction which we can then describe and attempt to explain. The whole process is much more from the inside looking out and less from the outside looking in. In other words, an *ad hoc* system is more likely to promote understanding and generate explanations than the system-based approaches discussed above. The fact that the instruments are designed in relation to a particular question or problem within a specific context makes the whole research process more meaningful and realistic. Perhaps most important of all is the fact that we are more likely to have confidence in the data.

The discussion now turns to a brief critique of discourse analysis as an approach to researching classroom interaction. The reader is referred to Chapter 2 for a summary of the main features of discourse analysis as a discipline.

5.2.2 Discourse analysis

Perhaps the earliest and most well-known proponents of discourse analysis (DA) in classrooms are Sinclair and Coulthard (1975) who, following a structural-functional linguistic route to analysis, compiled a list of 22 speech acts representing the verbal behaviours of both teachers and students participating in primary classroom communication. The outcome is the development of a descriptive system incorporating a discourse hierarchy:

LESSON
TRANSACTION
EXCHANGE
MOVE
ACT

Act is therefore the smallest discourse unit, while lesson is the largest; acts are described in terms of their discourse function, as in the two examples of speech acts below, *evaluation* and *cue*:

Extract 5.3

Act	Function	Realisation
Evaluation	evaluates	*right so it's like a rule* what do you mean?
Cue	evokes bid	yes *so tell me again* what you mean by that

One of the most important contributions of Sinclair and Coulthard to our understandings of classroom discourse is their realisation that most classroom discourse follows an IR(F) structure. For every move made by a student, teachers typically make two, as in:

I   T: what's the past tense of go?
R   S: went
F   T: went, excellent.

Thus, we can say that most teaching exchanges follow an IRF structure, made up of three moves, with each move containing one or more speech acts. Not only does this help to confirm the fact that teachers do speak much more than students in most classrooms, it also demonstrates how teachers often control the discourse. (For a full discussion of the IRF exchange, see Chapter 2).

The main difficulty associated with allocating utterances to functions is that any utterance can perform a range of functions. In a multi-party setting like a classroom, where there are so many things going on at the same time, deciding on a linguistic function may be extremely problematic. According to Stubbs (1983), it is almost impossible to say precisely what function is being performed by a teacher (or learner) act at any point in a lesson. As with most functional analyses, inside or outside a classroom, an utterance can have any number of functions depending on crucial contextual clues such as who said it, to whom, how they said it, why they said it and so on. Classification of classroom discourse in purely structural-functional terms is consequently problematic. Levinson (1983) takes up the same argument, stressing the fact that any one utterance can perform a multitude of functions, especially in a classroom setting where interaction patterns are so complex. The consequence of this is that there is no way, under speech act theory, to account for gestures or behavioural traits.

Discourse analysis, then, attempts to categorise naturally occurring patterns of interaction and account for them by reference to a discourse hierarchy. The starting point is structural-functional linguistics: classroom data are analysed according to their structural patterning and function. For example, the interrogative structure *'what time does this lesson end?'* could be interpreted as a request for information, an admonishment, a prompt or cue. Any attempt to analyse classroom data using a DA approach, therefore, involves some simplification and reduction. Matching utterances to categories may be problematic owing to the issues of multi-functionality and the absence of a direct relationship between form and function.

A more micro-analytic and naturalistic approach to classroom discourse is that offered by conversation analysis (again, see Chapter 2), whose origins lie in sociology rather than applied linguistics.

5.2.3 Conversation analysis

Conversation analysis is based on the premise that social contexts are not static but are constantly being formed by participants through their use of language and the ways in which turn-taking, openings and closures, sequencing of acts and so on are locally managed. Interaction is examined in relation to meaning and context; the way in which actions are sequenced is central to the process. In the words of Heritage:

> In fact, CA embodies a theory which argues that sequences of actions are a major part of what we mean by context, that the meaning of an action is heavily shaped by the sequence of previous actions from which it emerges, and that social context is a dynamically created thing that is expressed in and through the sequential organization of interaction. (1997: 162)

According to this view, interaction is *context-shaped* and *context-renewing*; that is, one contribution is dependent on a previous one and subsequent contributions create a new context for later actions. Under this microscopic view of context, one person's contribution is inextricably linked to that of another person. Order in spoken discourse is established through sequential organisation: the way in which one utterance is connected to another.

To see how this works in a classroom, consider extract 5.3 below. In the extract, every turn is uniquely linked to the previous and following ones and there is a clear sense that this represents a coherent piece of discourse which could have only occurred in a classroom context. Turns 187–199 make up a piece of spoken text which is coherent and logical because of the ways in which one turn is interdependent on another. The whole extract is a good example of a piece of discourse which is co-constructed by participants and which is shaped by a goal-oriented activity: here, eliciting the word *force*.

Extract 5.4

187	T:	=what do we call I'm going to try and get the class to tell you what
188		this word is that you're looking for … er we talk about military (claps hands)
189		… military what?
190	L:	((1))=

191	T:	=like fight=
192	L:	=kill=
193	T:	=no not [kill]]
194	L:	[action] action=
195	T:	=no ((2)) military?=
196	LL:	=power=
197	T:	=power think of another word military?
198	LL:	((3)) force=
199	T:	=so she believes in a FORCE for?
200	L:	that guide our lives=
201	T:	=that guides our lives=

Perhaps the most relevant strand of CA to the study of classroom discourse is that referred to as 'institutional discourse conversation analysis'. In any institution, the goals and actions of participants are closely linked to, and to some extent constrained by, the institutional business. In a language classroom, for example, most interactions are related to the enterprise of learning a second language; turn and topic management, sequential organisation and choice of lexis are all determined by that enterprise and by the roles of interactants. The interactions which take place in these contexts are largely shaped by the roles performed by the interactants and by the business of the moment. It comes as no surprise, therefore, that teachers typically ask questions and students (usually) answer them. What CA can do is to uncover something of the detail of these interactions by looking at the ways in which contexts are co-created in relation to the goal-oriented activity in which they are engaged (Heritage 1997: 163).

The main features of a CA approach to analysing L2 classroom interaction can be summarised as follows:

- The aim of CA is to account for the structural organisation of the interaction as determined by the participants. There should be no attempt to 'fit' the data to preconceived categories.
- The approach is strictly empirical. CA forces the researcher to focus on the interaction patterns emerging *from* the data, rather than relying on any preconceived notions which language practitioners may bring *to* the data (Seedhouse 2004).
- The observer is seen as a 'member' of the interaction, trying to view the experience through the eyes of the participants. The aim is to offer an emic (insider) perspective.
- Context is dynamic and mutually constructed by the participants. Contexts are therefore constantly changing as a lesson progresses and according to local demands and constraints.
- Talk is seen, in an institutional setting, as being goal-oriented: participants are striving towards some overall objective related to the institution. In a language classroom, for example, the discourse is influenced by the fact that all participants are focusing on some pre-determined aim, learning a second language.
- The analysis of the data is *multi-layered*. CA approaches emphasise both context and the sequentiality of utterances. Because no one utterance is categorised in

isolation and because contributions are examined in sequence, a CA methodology is much better equipped to interpret and account for the multi-layered structure of classroom interaction.

The discussion now turns to a brief overview of corpus-based approaches.

TASK 5.2
Based on what you now know about analysing classroom discourse, which approach might you choose and why? What difficulties would you expect to encounter and how might you overcome them?

5.3 CORPUS-BASED APPROACHES

A corpus is a collection of texts that is stored electronically on a computer or other form of electronic storage. These texts can be from written sources such as books, magazines, junk mail, letters, advertisements, business documents, literature, academic papers, emails and internet pages. A corpus can also be a collection of spoken texts, such as conversations, phone calls, speeches, TV chat shows, classrooms and so on. A corpus, therefore, is a collection of real language that people use in all types of situations. Using a corpus is not unlike using an internet search engine. It is essentially a large database which can be used to find every occurrence of a word or phrase. Just like an internet search, the 'hits' that result from your search will, in a matter of seconds, pop up on your screen. The use of specialist software such as 'Wordsmith Tools' (Scott 1996) enables searches to be conducted in a matter of seconds.

Although the trend in the early days of corpus linguistics was for large corpora, an interesting development in recent years is that it is now becoming increasingly common for researchers to use much smaller corpora of around 50–100,000 words. The reason for this is that these smaller corpora are usually highly context specific and applied to address a particular problem. It is not difficult, for example, to see how a small corpus of around 50,000 words of university small group talk could be usefully applied to look at the ways in which local and international students interact in seminars. Here, a small corpus has been used to address a 'real world problem' in a very useful and illuminating way. The reason this approach works is that all the data are recorded in a single, homogeneous context and used in response to a particular question or problem. The corpus is not simply descriptive, but pro-active in relation to a particular issue.

Essentially, then, we are more concerned with what a corpus can do rather than what it is (Biber et al. 1998; Sinclair 1997). Corpus linguistics (CL), in the present context, should be viewed as a *methodological tool* which will help us to gain a closer understanding of classroom discourse. CL has been used in this way in a range of contexts where the *use* of language is the focus of empirical study. Such contexts include courtrooms and forensic linguistics (Cotterill 2010), the workplace (Koester

2006), the classroom and educational contexts (O'Keeffe and Farr 2003, Walsh and O'Keeffe 2007), political discourse (Ädel 2010), advertising and the media (O'Keeffe 2006), among other areas. In all of these cases, CL is used as a methodological tool and another approach, such as CA (see below), is drawn on as a framework.

CL has at its disposal a range of techniques which can be used for the study of classroom discourse. These are discussed briefly below.

5.3.1 Concordancing

Concordancing uses corpus software to find every occurrence of a particular word or phrase. The search word or phrase is often referred to as the *node* and concordance lines are usually presented with the node word/phrase in the centre of the line with seven or eight words presented at either side. These are known as Key-Word-In-Context displays (or 'KWIC' concordances). Concordance lines challenge us to read in an entirely new way, vertically, or even from the centre outwards in both directions. They are usually scanned vertically at first glance, that is, looked at up or down the central pattern, along the line of the node word or phrase. Here are some sample lines from a concordance of the word *way* using the Limerick Corpus of Irish English (LCIE) taken from O'Keeffe et al. (2007):

Ireland is no different in a *way* then em what they were
of you anyhow? Now in a *way* 'What Dreams may come' it's
in college in fact it's a *way* of life and you find this
he present things in such a *way* that he would persuade
of life is to live in such a *way* that when you die your soul
he obviously lived a certain *way* of live and they wanted to
to deal with in a different *way* they couldn't deal with it
stadium that's the easiest *way* to describe it. There is a
find this the most effective *way*. Ok now today em you have as
there is no evidence either *way*. You can't have evidence
from the top and works his *way* down. The theologian will
so it speaks and works its *way* up. The theologian starts

Our concordance analysis of this extract reveals the following:

- *Way* frequently co-occurs with the preposition *in* (*in a way*, *in no way*, etc.).
- It is often used to form fixed or semi-fixed phrases (*in a way*, *on the way*, *a way of life*, *in such a way*, etc.).
- *Way* is frequently followed by another preposition (*to*, *down*, *up*, etc.).
- It occurs more frequently in the middle of a clause than at the beginning or end.

Concordance line analysis is very productive in terms of looking at language patterning such as idiomatic usages or collocation. In a classroom setting, it could be a very fruitful means of gaining detailed understandings of, for example, the use of discourse markers or question sequences (for a detailed illustration see O'Keeffe et al. 2007).

5.3.2 Word frequency counts or word lists

Another common corpus technique which software can perform is the extremely rapid calculation of word frequency lists (or word lists) for any batch of texts. By running a word frequency list on a corpus, you get a rank ordering of all the words in order of frequency. This function facilitates enquiry across different corpora, different language varieties and different contexts of use. Below, for example are the first ten words from three very different spoken corpora:

A. Service encounters: a sub-corpus of the Limerick Corpus of Irish English (LCIE) comprising shop encounters (8,500 words).
B. Friends chatting: a sub-corpus of LCIE, consisting of female friends chatting (40,000 words).
C. Academic English: The Limerick-Belfast Corpus of Academic Spoken English (LIBEL CASE, one million words of Academic English).

Even from the first ten most frequent words, we can see differing patterns of use (any of these words can then be concordanced to look at how they are functioning in the texts):

	A	B	C
1	You	I	The
2	Of	And	And
3	Is	The	Of
4	Thanks	To	You
5	It	Was	To
6	I	You	A
7	Please	It	That
8	The	Like	In
9	Yeah	That	It
10	Now	He	Is

(Walsh and O'Keeffe 2007)

From this very brief extract, we can make the following observations: The shop (column 1) and casual conversation (column 2) results show markers of interactivity typical of spoken English such as *I, you, yeah* (as a response token), *like, please, and thanks* (see Carter and McCarthy 2006). The first ten words of the academic corpus (3) lack the interactive markers found in first two columns. The academic corpus has more of the features of a written text such as a high frequency of articles, *a* and *the*, use of the preposition *of*, use of *that*.

Again, there are many other observations which we could make from this data. The point is that CL allows us to make important and reliable observations from our data very quickly.

5.3.3 Key word analysis

This function allows us to identify the key words in one or more texts. Key words, as detailed by Scott (1996), are those whose frequency is unusually high in comparison with some norm. Key words are not usually the most frequent words in a text (or collection of texts), rather they are the more 'unusually frequent' (Scott 1996). Software compares two pre-existing word lists and one of these is assumed to be a large word list which will act as a reference file or benchmark corpus. The other is the word list based on the text(s) which you want to study. The larger corpus will provide background data for reference comparison. For example, we saw above that *the* is the most frequent word in the LIBEL corpus of spoken academic English (see above). Scott notes that the key word facility provides a useful way of characterising a text or a genre and has potential applications in the areas of forensic linguistics, stylistics, content analysis and text retrieval. In the context of language teaching, it can be used by teachers and materials writers to create word lists, for example in Languages for Specific Purposes programmes (e.g., English for Pilots).

5.3.4 Cluster analysis

The analysis of how language systematically clusters into combinations of words or *chunks* (e.g., *I mean, this that and the other*, etc.) can give insights into how we describe the vocabulary of a language (Wray 2000, 2002; McCarthy and Carter 2002). As O'Keeffe et al. (2007) note, the way in which words cluster together into chunks has implications for what we teach in our vocabulary lessons and how learners approach the task of acquiring vocabulary and developing fluency. As a corpus technique, the process of generating chunks or cluster lists is similar to making single word frequency lists. Instead of asking thecomputer to rank all of the single words in the corpus in order of frequency, we can ask it to look for word combinations, for example 2-, 3-, 4-, 5-, or 6-word combinations. For example, using *Wordsmith Tools*, here are the 12 most frequent 3-word combinations from the LIBEL corpus of academic spoken English:

1. *A lot of*
2. *And so on*
3. *I don't know*
4. *At the moment*
5. *In other words*
6. *A number of*
7. *A couple of*
8. *A little bit*
9. *A bit of*
10. *As I said*
11. *First of all*
12. *As well as*

(Walsh and O'Keeffe 2007)

What is interesting from this cluster analysis from a classroom discourse perspective is the frequency of words and phrases which are used to 'point' in the discourse and to locate learning in time and place. Phrases like *as I said, first of all, in other words* perform an important signposting function and enable learners to find their way through the discourse; such signposting is essential to prevent learners from becoming lost. Effective teachers use discourse markers naturally and almost without thinking.

In this section, I have outlined the main benefits of a corpus linguistics approach to the study of classroom discourse and highlighted its main advantages in terms of speed and accessibility of data and reliability of findings. In the next section, I consider how CL might combine with other approaches, especially CA.

5.4 CLCA: CORPUS LINGUISTICS AND CONVERSATION ANALYSIS

While CL offers a very useful means of portraying the general patterns and trends in a corpus, it cannot offer the kind of fine-grained, detailed analysis which CA gives. While a CL analysis allows us to make generalisations about word frequencies and collocations, it does not permit us to get close to the interaction and to see how interlocutors really communicate. In order to conduct a detailed analysis of the discourse, I propose that CL can usefully be combined with conversation analysis (CA), an established and respected approach to providing detailed, micro-analytic descriptions of spoken interaction. This combined approach, using both CL and CA (henceforth, CLCA) cumulatively gives a more 'up-close' description of spoken interactions in an educational setting than that offered by using either one on its own. From the analysis, we can gain powerful insights into the ways in which interactants establish understandings and observe how words, utterances and text combine in the co-construction of meaning.

In the previous section, the point was made that the current trend in corpus-based approaches to the study of discourse is towards smaller, more specialised and context specific corpora. Arguably, such corpora lend themselves to multiple layers of analysis and provide opportunities for combining different methodologies. Previously, when it was 'fashionable' to only construct large corpora, the main focus was on lexical patterning rather than discourse context because 'large corpora were lexically rich but contextually poor' (Walsh et al., 2010). That is, when researchers look at a lexical item in a 100 million word corpus, they are detached from its context. However, when researchers record, transcribe, annotate and build a small, contextualised spoken corpus, a different landscape of the possibilities opens up in areas beyond lexis to areas of use (especially issues of pragmatics, interaction and discourse).

When we consider the potential value of combining CL with CA, it may appear that they have very little in common in terms of their approach to analysis. CL deals with large texts and pays little attention to context, whereas CA looks at the microscopic details of shorter texts which are highly contextualised. CA uses a qualitative analysis, CL's is quantitative. The main focus of CL is lexis: single words, combinations of words, word clusters. CA, on the other hand, is more interested in turns: sequential organisations, sequencing, shifts and so on. With this said, however, in fact both CA and CL have a number of features which link them:

- Both use a corpus of empirical data.
- Both refer to baseline comparisons with other types of interactions (canonical sequential order in the case of CA, reference corpora in CL).
- CA offers an emic, close-up perspective, CL complements by providing a bigger picture.
- Both start from the data and work outwards to construct context (from turn order in CA, from patterns in CL).
- Both attach importance to lexis in creation of meanings (though this is down-played in CA)
- Word patterns (CL) often lead to consistent turn patterns (CA).

How might a combined CLCA approach be used in the study of classroom discourse? The following example may help to illustrate this. In a study on small group teaching in Irish universities, Walsh et al. (2010) used a combined CLCA approach in order to provide 'thick' descriptions of spoken interaction. The authors argue that this combined approach enables features of spoken discourse to be described at both micro (word) and macro (text) levels. A CLCA methodology reveals the relationships between interaction patterns and lexical chunks. By looking at sequences of turns alongside, for example, discourse markers, new levels of understanding can be reached, the authors claimed. As the authors themselves say:

> This approach to analysis provides powerful insights into the ways in which interactants establish understandings in educational settings and, in particular, highlights the inter-dependency of words, utterances and text in the co-construction of meaning. (Walsh et al. 2010: 48)

The following extract from the same study illustrates some of the merits of a combined CLCA approach.

Extract 5.5

```
 1   T:    how are you getting on with your other ahh module (.)
 2         ahh the the the filming one
 3   S3:   we're filming a scene at the moment we're editing and
 4         it's crazy
 5   T:    yeah you see it is crazy isn't it (.) this week now
 6         is going to be unbelievable
 7   S3:   it's just music and we're just putting it together
 8         you see now (.) you know you've all the footage but
 9         you're there trying
10   S?:   ( )
11   S3    we have so much footage and it's just like you some
12         people have to accept that some of it
```

```
13   S?    ( )
14   T:    yeah well it's like essays isn't it (.) I mean you
15         can't write from the middle you know=
16   S4    =that was my idea so we can't lose that and you're
17         like going=
18   T:    =who who's the director?
19   S3    I wish I was the director
20   S2    in our in my group John C is
21   T:    okay yeah you see that's the thing like you know I
22         mean like really it does all come down to the
23         director and the people should respect that
24         immediately you know (.) that doesn't happen that
25         often (.) you know what I mean it can get the roles
26         can get dispersed
```

(Walsh et al. 2010)

This extract is taken from a module on 'film studies'. One of the striking features which emerged from the quantitative analysis (CL) of the corpus were the high frequencies of *you know* and *you see* (highlighted in extract 5.5). These discourse markers are used frequently in classrooms in order to create 'shared space' where learning can occur. According to Carter and McCarthy (2006), *you see* usually marks new information while *you know* generally marks shared information. In this study, there were significant differences in the frequencies of *you know* and *you see* when compared with a corpus of everyday talk (see Figure 1).

The interesting point here is that in the corpus of higher education discourse, we find an exceptional number *you knows* (marking shared information) but we find more or less the same amount of *you sees* (marking new information). The priority to build on and appeal to shared knowledge and 'shared space' is central to both the pedagogic and the interactional process. In extract 5.5, the same result is borne out. There are a large number of occurrences of both *you see* and *you know*, but it is evident that *you know* is used much more frequently in order to establish common ground, create shared space, demonstrate empathy between tutor and students and create a sense that 'we're all in this together; I'm here to help you.'

From this linguistic analysis of the extract (using CL), we now turn to an analysis of the interaction (using CA). Our analysis of the interaction in extract 5.5 reveals the following:

- Turns are evenly distributed and fairly symmetrical: it is not immediately obvious who the tutor is.
- Students manage the turn-taking independently of the tutor in a way which is similar to casual conversation.
- In response to the teacher's opening turn, one student (S3) produces an account of a group's experiences of making a film, including an assessment of the situation (it's crazy), to which the tutor offers a preferred (agreeing) response

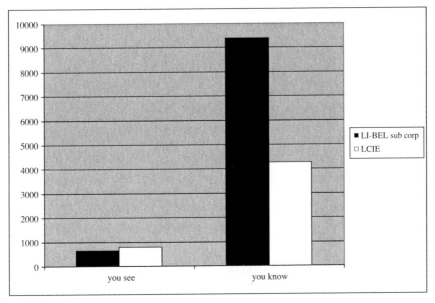

Figure 5.1   Comparison of 'you see' and 'you know' in LI-BEL sub corpus and
LCIE (normalised results)

with the discourse marker 'yeah' and the repetition of the assessment, before
building on this to project what experiences will be like in the future.

- In lines 11 and 12, S3 indicates that 'some people' may have problems in accepting that material has to be cut, and in line 19 seems to be expressing frustration
  either about the existing director, or the lack of a director's role in the group.
- Throughout this extract, the tutor takes students' experiences and feelings and
  builds on them, thus orienting to a pedagogic goal of reinforcing appropriate
  behaviours and identities in the context of professional practice. Throughout,
  the tutor plays a more or less equal role, listening attentively, as indicated by the
  use of acknowledgement tokens (in lines 5, 14 and 21).
- A lot of pragmatic work takes place in lines 21–26, where *okay* marks a switch
  in orientation, and the tutor switches roles from empathic listener to tutor. Here,
  there is a lot of interactional work in order to change footing (Goffman 1981):
  okay yeah you see that's the thing like you know I mean like really. His stance after
  this preface is that of teacher again, giving instruction and passing on new
  knowledge. The interactional work is apparently needed in order to change from
  equal interactant to tutor, to move from a position of role symmetry to one of
  role asymmetry.

In the preceding analysis and discussion, I have tried to demonstrate that CL and CA
can be usefully combined in any study of classroom discourse. Not only are they
mutually beneficial, they actually offer each other synergies and enable a deeper,

richer level of analysis. The approach is iterative: it requires a switch from CL to CA, back to CL and then on to further CA. One approach informs the other, provides direction and enables closer analysis. For example, the frequency counts of *you know* and *you see* alone do not provide the whole picture. Looking at how they actually operate in a piece of interaction gives a much fuller 'flavour' of the relationship between linguistic forms and interactional features. More importantly, this combined analysis gives real insights into how people communicate in an educational setting. Had this study used CL on its own, it would have achieved interesting lists of high frequency items but it would not have brought us anywhere near the depth of understanding offered by a CA framework. Similarly, if the data had been viewed from a purely CA perspective, the analysis would have identified some interesting interactional features but overlooked the high frequencies of certain items and ignored how specific lexical features operate in the interaction.

5.5 SUMMARY

The aim of this chapter was to present alternative approaches for studying classroom interaction, beginning with corpus linguistics. The main advantage of CL is that it offers rapid and reliable profiles of classroom discourse and enables us to understand how linguistic features 'work' in specific classroom contexts. For example, I commented on the ways in which discourse markers (such as *you know, you see, right, ok, next*, etc.) perform key functions in classrooms and, when used properly, greatly assist the learning process. CL's main disadvantage is that it largely ignores the finer details of classroom interaction and fails to recognise the ways in which meanings are jointly achieved. A combined CLCA approach was proposed as one way of overcoming such shortcomings, allowing a 'multi-layered' perspective which offers a description of both linguistic and interactional features.

In the final section of this chapter, I presented a brief summary of the work which has been done to promote variable approaches to analysing classroom interaction. Here, there is a recognition that classroom discourse cannot be viewed as being 'all of a oneness', where interactional and linguistic features occur in a more or less fixed and predictable way. Instead, variable approaches recognise that classroom interaction proceeds in line with the pedagogic goals of the moment. Micro-contexts are co-constructed in the interaction as participants work towards clearly defined, and constantly shifting, goals. So, for example, if the teacher's goal is to set up a pair-work task, she may use long teacher turns, frequent pausing, specific discourse markers (such as *first, next, then*) and so on. If, on the other hand, her aim is to elicit student opinions, there may be longer learner turns, more role asymmetry, frequent overlaps, interruptions and false starts – in short, the interaction will resemble more closely a casual conversation.

Recognising that classroom discourse is constantly shifting, that goals are always changing and that language use and pedagogic goals must work together is, I suggest, fundamental to teacher development. One of the most effective means of developing as a teacher is to gain closer understandings of classroom interaction: using the types of research tools presented in this chapter might be the first step towards enhanced understandings of interactional processes which in turn will result in improved teaching and learning.

Chapter 6

Reflective practice revisited

The aim of this chapter is to revisit the construct reflective practice by making the argument that there is a need to approach RP in a more considered and structured way. One way of doing this is to place classroom discourse at the centre of the process and to make interaction the focus of reflections. In short, I will argue that reflective practice isn't 'working' in its present guise and that it should be revisited and revitalised. In the discussion which follows, I give my reasons for this claim, arguing that the notion of reflective practice has become tired, overused and outdated. Although I do not question the need for RP and wholeheartedly endorse it as a key component of professional practice, I argue here that it is currently only operating in a limited, rather superficial way. In order to ensure that it is an active professional practice which has impact, I suggest that we should make classroom discourse the main focus; that professionals need to have something to reflect *on*; that we need some kind of evidence to *inform* our reflections; and that RP works best when it is done through *dialogue*, preferably with a colleague.

Each of these arguments will be developed in the discussion which follows. The first part of the chapter offers a critique of RP, identifying some of the key issues which have emerged over recent years; in the second part, I suggest a way forward by revisiting reflective practice.

TASK 6.1
What do you understand by the term *reflective practice*? Have you ever reflected on your practice? How did you do it and what was the end result?

6.1 DEFINITIONS OF REFLECTIVE PRACTICE

The notion of reflective practice has been around for many years, beginning with the work of Dewey in 1933, who made the case for the importance of experiential learning accompanied by reflective thought. His main argument was that any professional development is dependent on a detailed understanding of interaction, experience and reflection: a position which coincides very much with the one being advocated here.

My argument is that, in order to engage in professional development, we need to begin by focusing on classroom interaction.

Dewey's work was later developed by Schön (1983, 1996), who differentiated between reflection-in-action and reflection-on-action. While both are relevant, the former is concerned essentially with thought accompanied by action, while the latter is concerned with reflection after action. In a classroom, so much of what constitutes 'good teaching' is linked to the decisions made while teaching, what I call 'online decision-making'. It could be argued that these reflections in action lie at the heart of effective teaching and that we should be helping teachers to make good interactive decisions which promote learning. It is also true, however, that reflection after the event, post-teaching, is central to any long-term professional development. For this reason, both are addressed in this chapter. More recently, Killion and Todnem (1991) advocate 'reflection-for-action' in an endeavour to make the process more continuous and more structured, ideas which again are central to the present discussion.

Defining RP is problematic, leading Russell to conclude 'one reason for the under-valuing of reflection as a skill lies in the lack of a universally agreed definition of what constitutes reflection' (2005: 48). This position is echoed by others such as Griffiths (2000) and Mackintosh (1998) who argue that RP is ambiguous, misused and 'of unproven benefit'. The discussion which follows concurs with the position of Boud et al. who assert that reflection is a process of 'turning experience into learning' (1985: 7). Their definition is the one which has most resonance here. They say that reflective practice is: 'a generic term for those intellectual and affective activities in which individuals engage to explore their experiences in order to lead to new understandings and appreciation' (1985: 3). Like many others, their definition emphasises the importance of 'action' and 'criticality', both of which seem pertinent to the position adopted throughout this book. That is, professional development requires both action – from the perspective of learning from one's behaviour – and criticality – in that we need to adopt a critical stance to the professional work we undertake. This is not the same as being critical; rather, criticality refers to a need for greater objectivity which is evidence-based.

Despite the diversity of definitions and wide-ranging disagreement, RP is, I believe, still worthy of study and promotion. In the next section, I outline some of the issues associated with its present status before turning to consider a possible way forward.

6.2 THE 'PROBLEMS' OF REFLECTIVE PRACTICE

In addition to the problems associated with definition outlined in the previous section, a number of practitioners have argued that RP has become a tired and over-used construct and one which may have exhausted its usefulness. Bradbury et al. (2010), for example, claim that there is now a pressing need to identify new approaches to CPD (continuing professional development) by moving 'beyond reflective practice'. Others, like Boud (2010), suggest that too many educational practices are currently being advocated as examples of reflection. Indeed, perhaps one of the key issues at stake is the fact that there are too many models of reflection. Too often, when reading accounts of reflection, there is a sense that we should follow a particular model which incorporates some kind of linear progression; the idea that if we do X then Y then Z, there will be an improvement in professional practice. Nowhere, to my knowledge, do any of these models actually *teach* us how to do reflective practice. The teaching – and associated problem of assessment – of reflective practice has been taken up by a number of writers. Russell, for example, states that RP 'can and should be taught –explicitly, directly, thoughtfully and patiently—using personal reflection-in-action to interpret and improve one's teaching of reflective practice to others' (2005: 204). Alger (2006) proposes that reflection could be fostered through activities such as action research, case studies, microteaching and reflective writing assignments. Park (2003) has identified reflective journals as potentially valuable tools for developing critically reflective practitioners. He claimed that the journaling process did a number of things including stimulating critical thinking, allowing teacher educators some insights into the minds of the candidates, and helping the candidates to understand better the process of learning.

At the same time, caution has been expressed concerning the assessment of reflections. Hobbs identified some problems with reflective journals that were assessed and suggested that reflections should not be assessed in the early stages but only after individuals have had significant experience. She went on to provide suggestions for gaining that experience (2007: 415). Hargreaves (2004), however, argued that requiring reflection for assessment purposes may not be a positive learning strategy and that reflections should be required but not assessed. Both positions are taken up in this chapter (see below), where I argue the case for *oral* reflections rather than written ones.

A number of models of reflection have been advocated and are currently actively used. Perhaps the most influential is Kolb's (1984) model of experiential learning which demonstrates how, in any reflective cycle, we move from concrete experience, through reflective (self)-observation, to a theoretical position and then on to active experimentation. The whole cycle then repeats, as shown in Figure 6.1.

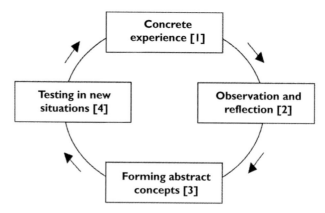

Figure 6.1   Kolb's experiential learning cycle

Although there may be some value in representing reflection in this diagrammatic, cyclical manner, there are also inherent dangers. The main concern is that models such as the one described above are open to interpretations which may be too literal. It may be, for example, that we all go through a different series of steps, or that we do not follow the precise sequence indicated. Of more serious concern is the fact that we may be inclined to 'go through the motions' of reflection without engaging in it in any meaningful or reflexive sense. Burns (2005) makes a similar point, arguing for RP to be viewed as a series of inter-related practices rather than a series of steps which must be followed.

A related danger associated with models of reflection is that the model becomes the centrepiece of the institution's philosophy about RP. This is often the case on initial teacher education programmes (see Harris 2013) and may result in RP being viewed as an institutional requirement, as part of student-teachers' assessment rather than as a tool to help them in their professional practice. This is clearly borne out in the quote below:

> Sometimes I don't really see the relevancy [sic] to reflect on some of the assignments we do, and therefore, really, all I'm doing is I am writing up something that may or may not be my actual opinion, I'm just writing something up to hand something in. I find that happens more often than maybe you'd like. (McCabe et al. 2011: 68)

There is more than a hint in the above quote from a trainee teacher on a Canadian initial teacher education programme that this person fails to see the relevance of written reflections which are submitted as an assignment and assessed. One of the dangers of overusing models is precisely this: they become the focus of the reflection, not the means of accomplishing it. Essentially, doing the writing, or completing the assignment is equated with doing reflection. Rather than focusing on reflection, participants devote all their energy to completing the task, resulting in inauthentic reflection (Roberts 1998) or even 'faking it' (Hobbs 2007). The upshot is that, through written reflections using pro-forma, checklists or journals, teachers operate at a 'surface' level, failing to engage with the process of reflection and even becoming disenchanted with the process. Criticality and subsequent professional actions do not even feature in this process of 'lip-service reflection'. For many, especially trainees on initial teacher education courses, the repeated use of the same instrument for reflection (checklist, pro-forma, etc.) may have the effect of actually stunting professional development. Rather than using the same reflective task, there is a need for graded reflection, where trainees are asked to complete a different task according to their stage of development. The use of graded written reflections is, arguably, more likely to result in engaged activity and professional development.

Despite these criticisms of written reflections, there is a counter argument. A more discursive approach to writing is potentially evidence of the reflection itself. Putting thoughts on paper and composing a critical self-observation is a valuable and potentially powerful means of promoting reflection. The act of writing itself entails a process of thinking, composing and restating a position. It involves clarifying for the writer a recent experience and considering alternative future actions. This kind of reflection, I suggest, is to be encouraged and might usefully replace some of the more 'tick-box' types of task currently used on pre-service teacher education programmes.

In the remainder of this section, I describe three problems associated with current approaches to RP. Possible ways of dealing with each problem are then discussed in the next section, using arguments which have been presented in earlier chapters.

I have already argued that while RP has considerable merit in initial and in-service teacher education, it has the following shortcomings (see also Walsh 2006; Mann and Walsh 2013):

- It is not data-led and lacks the evidence needed to make decisions about professional practice.
- It is often regarded as an individual task or process, which undervalues the importance of collaboration and dialogue with others.
- It does not always make use of the most appropriate tools for engaging in reflection.

6.2.1 The need for data

There are at least two reasons for the need for data-led accounts of RP. First, most reports of reflective practice do not include any evidence of people actually *doing* reflection (but see Farr 2011; Harris 2013). In order to understand the processes of RP and assess its impact and relevance, there needs to be a sustained and structured approach to data-collection which shows what reflection looks like in practice. Future research on RP should include evidence in the form of recorded reflective sessions, spoken interactions, video-recorded feedback sessions from teaching practicums and so on. Only by capturing the finer details of reflection-in-action will researchers and practitioners gain the kind of understanding needed to help us progress.

Consider the following two extracts, taken from focus group data recorded in an international comparative study of RP conducted in Northern Ireland and Canada (see McCabe et al. 2011). Both extracts include a response to the question 'what do you understand by reflective practice?' Extract 6.1 is one student-teacher's response, while 6.2 is the response by one teacher educator.

Extract 6.1
[RP is] looking back over what you have accomplished and looking at areas of strengths and weaknesses and what you might want to change the next time that you do it .

Extract 6.2
Looking at the experiences we bring to the classroom like images of other teachers, experiences that they've had that they don't even recognise impact upon their practice, and so when I say going deeper with reflective practice, I mean really taking a look at the stories that they bring to the classroom and how that impacts on what they do every day as opposed to just what went well and what didn't go well.

The differences between the position adopted by the student-teacher and that taken by their trainer are not difficult to detect. In the first extract we see how concerned this student is with the actual daily mechanics of teaching. There is a sense that RP is concerned with looking at today and doing it better tomorrow, a position which is completely understandable and widespread in initial teacher education. Compare this perspective, however, with that of the academic, the teacher educator, who takes a much broader view of RP, based on the 'lived experiences' of the trainees. There might be some debate around these two positions: how ready, for example, are pre-service teachers to investigate in detail their lived experiences? Should reflection at this stage not be more about 'survival'? The participants' responses appear to fit into two distinct categories; while the students overwhelmingly refer to RP as a response to an event or a series of events, faculty see it as a continuum whereby teachers undergo a process of understanding where they have come from and how this impacts on their effectiveness as teachers. While both perspectives are clearly valid, the important point I am making here is that we need data in order to show this. Even at the level of 'what is RP?' there will be different perspectives which need to be understood and discussed.

The second issue relating to a lack of data is that the process of reflection itself requires evidence (in the form of data). While we can all certainly usefully reflect on our experiences while teaching, having actual evidence (a recording, feedback from a colleague, a conversation with a student) will greatly facilitate reflection, making it both deeper and longer-lasting. If student-teachers were taught from day one of a teacher education programme how to collect data and what we mean by data, think how much richer their experience as trainees might be; consider too how much more likely they are to become researchers of their own practice throughout their career. Most professional decisions in all walks of life are based on evidence: why should RP be any different?

6.2.2 RP as an individual activity

If, for most adults, learning (and this includes professional development) is regarded as an active, problem-based and interactive process, why is RP so often conducted in isolation? For many, this entails thinking about teaching before a lesson, conducting the lesson and then reflecting on it afterwards, all done as individual activities. There is little or no dialogue or discussion and very little sharing or understanding of key issues which might emerge. The view taken here is that the process should be a joint, collaborative one, entailing spoken interactions rather than written reflections. It is a view shared by others, notably Johns (2000) who emphasises the act of sharing with a colleague or mentor, which enables the experience to be understood at a faster rate than through reflection alone. Brookfield too suggests that critically reflective teachers should make use of the 'critical reflective lenses of the students' eyes, our colleagues' experiences, and theoretical literature' in their reflections on practice (1997: 234).

The current position of RP is perhaps surprising when we consider that most theories of learning stress its social and collaborative dimensions, and when teachers are being encouraged to engage students in dialogue and discussion (cf. Alexander 2008). It is proposed in the second part of the chapter that RP must adopt a more interactive and dialectic stance if it is to survive and prosper.

6.2.3 A lack of appropriate tools

One of the major problems associated with RP in its current state is that it rarely offers tools which help practitioners to reflect on their practice. In addition to the fact that many of the tools currently available advocate a written reflective response (see previous discussion), associated problems include the fact that some tools being used were designed for and by researchers and are not necessarily appropriate, while others tend to adopt a 'one-size fits all' approach which fails to take account of local context. As we have seen above, on pre-service courses reflective tools need to be introduced gradually and in a timely manner so that student-teachers are taught how to reflect and what to reflect on over time. Repeated use of the same instrument, for example, should be avoided at all costs, as should tasks which are too complicated.

To illustrate these arguments, consider extract 6.3 below. This is taken from the same Canadian study cited above (McCabe et al. 2011). Here, we witness the comments of one trainee teacher who has been asked how she reflects.

> **Extract 6.3**
> One of the things that I really enjoyed was the assignment where we actually did our own personal teaching philosophy why we thought we were here, and after we went through the year, we went back and reflected on what we said originally. I think that was really important to see how you've grown as a teacher and really whether or not you're in the right profession. I think of the assignment and I think that the faculty guidance in analysing it was very important. Listening to others' stories and their changes in the class was great!

A number of observations can be made from this extract. First, it is interesting to note that certain types of written reflection do have value, but that they tend to be of the discursive, narrative variety (*the assignment where we actually did our own teaching philosophy*). As an assignment, this has the potential to link teachers' beliefs, cognitions and lived experiences together, providing a unique opportunity for genuine, deep thinking about teaching practice. Second, there is the valuable observation that reflecting on previous introspections has considerable merit in order to gauge how we all change over time, especially true in a professional development context (*we went back and reflected on what we said originally*). Third, this trainee comments on the value of oral reflection and sharing of 'stories' as a useful means of promoting fuller, more engaged critical thinking about practice.

A final observation is that there is a sense in which many of the tools currently used in RP are often designed with the institution in mind, rather than with a focus on practitioners. There is evidence to suggest that RP is often seen as an institutional requirement, as yet another piece of administration which has to be completed, rather than as a tool which is designed to aid professional growth. The kinds of forms, checklists, pro-formas and 'assignments' currently being used on pre-service teacher education programmes may not always be trainee-centred, designed instead with the practices, systems and procedures of the organisation in mind (cf. Gray and Block 2012). Instead, we need tools which are designed with the trainee in mind, which reflect the local context and which vary according to stage of development. This will be picked up in the second part of the chapter.

So far, we have seen that RP favours written over spoken forms, is perceived as an institutional requirement rather than a professional practice, lacks data, is conducted by individuals acting alone, and fails to make use of appropriate tools. I am not claiming that these problems of RP prevail in every context, nor am I saying that this is an exhaustive list. Rather, my argument is that these are typical concerns across a range of contexts. In the next section, possible solutions to these issues are presented and discussed.

TASK 6.2

Based on the discussion so far and considering your own context, what issues in your own teaching would you like to reflect on? Write three questions and then decide how you would go about collecting evidence that would help you answer each question.

6.3 REFLECTIVE PRACTICE REVITALISED

In this section, I consider a possible way forward for RP by proposing that it should become more data-led, more dialogic and make better use of appropriate tools. Throughout, the concern is to look at ways of refocusing the reflective process by considering the importance of interaction – not just in the classroom but between teachers engaged in their own reflections in a teacher development setting. The case for a revitalisation of RP, I suggest, is essential if it is to become more widely used by teachers across their entire careers and not just within the confines of initial or in-service teacher education programmes. Rather than seeing RP as something which practitioners *must* do in order to meet the requirements of a teacher education programme, the aim is to consider how it might become a practice that professionals *want* to engage in as part of their regular working lives.

6.3.1 Data-led RP

In the previous section, I presented the case for a more evidence-based approach to reflection, under which key decisions or changes to professional practice are informed by data. One of the ways in which RP practices and procedures could be made more principled and objective is to make the whole process data-led. If we accept that there is far more to teacher education than skills training, we should recognise that teachers need to be equipped with the tools that will enable them to find out about their own classrooms and make adjustments (Bartlett 1990).

Perhaps one way of preparing teachers to engage in data-led reflection is to help them to become researchers of their own practice by taking part in action research, which is based on the premise that teachers can and should investigate their own classrooms (Cohen et al. 2011: 226). The starting point is the identification of a puzzle or issue; the process continues with data collection, data analysis, and finally outcomes – in the form of changes to practice – are suggested. Action research is typically a collaborative process, which entails discussion and dialogue with a colleague. Improvement or changes to teaching practice arise through the collection and analysis of a small amount of data and the subsequent discussions which take place.

According to Carr and Kemmis, action research can be defined as: 'a form of self-reflective inquiry undertaken by participants in social situations in order to improve the rationality and justice of their own practices, their understanding of these practices, and the situations in which the practices are carried out' (1983: 220–1). Cohen et al. (2011) identify eight stages in the process:

1. Identify the problem, or issue.
2. Develop a draft proposal.
3. Review what has already been written on the issue.
4. Restate the problem or formulate a hypothesis.
5. Select research procedures.
6. Choose evaluation procedures.
7. Collect data, analyse the data and provide feedback.
8. Interpret the data and make inferences.

Many practitioners may find the idea of collecting data alien or unnecessary. After all, they are teachers, not researchers and have little or no time to devote to data collection. And yet, when we consider what is meant by data, teachers have an enormous capacity to collect evidence: 'data' in this context are things like recordings of a teaching session, a set of test results, feedback from a colleague who has observed a teaching session, a conversation with a group of students, short, written feedback papers from students, a piece of material, a critical incident and so on. In short, collecting data means collecting evidence which will help a teacher address a particular issue. In the words of Johnson 'The more research-driven knowledge teachers have, the better their teaching performances will be' (1995: 29).

There are, then, huge differences between the kind of data collected in an action research project and that collected in a full research project. Data collected via action research is private rather than public, small- rather than large-scale, highly context specific. Data collected in this way, importantly, belongs to the teacher-researcher. Perhaps one of the most compelling reasons for encouraging data-led RP is that of ownership. I would argue that ownership of the data is the single most important factor contributing to enhanced understanding and professional development.

Ownership of the data is, arguably, far more likely to result in a change in teaching behaviour since one of the stages in getting teachers to modify their teaching behaviour is for them to *experience* the change: 'It's no good talking about or imposing change ... you have to let the changees experience what you are talking about first' (Harmer 1999: 5). Because teacher-researchers are both the producers and consumers of their research (Kumaravadivelu 1999), since they own the data and are responsible for effecting changes to classroom practices, the process is more private and, arguably, less intimidating.

The notion of developing understandings of context has been highlighted more than once in this chapter and elsewhere in the book, and I have made the point that an understanding of context is the most important first step in any teacher development programme. Van Lier terms this 'ecological research', drawing comparisons with any natural environment in which the slightest change in one sub-system will impact other systems: 'Ecological research pays a great deal of attention to the smallest detail of the interaction, since within these details maybe contained the seeds of learning. The reflective teacher can learn to "read" the environment to notice such details' (2000: 11). An ecological research project, then, studies interactional processes, paying attention to the slightest detail which may influence teaching and learning. Teachers work very closely with the data they collect in their own context, their own 'environment', to use van Lier's term. The advantage of this approach is that there is a unification of theory and practice since the smallest details can be studied, changes implemented and then evaluated (van Lier 2000). The main reason for the potential for such microscopic analysis is the fact that the research is located in a context which is both clearly defined and familiar to the teacher-researcher.

One of the tenets of action research is that it entails collaboration and dialogue (Kemmis and McTaggart 1992). Dialogue is a crucial part of the reflection-action-further-reflection cycle, since it allows for clarification, questioning and ultimately enhanced understanding. Conversation is the means by which new ideas are expressed, doubts aired and concerns raised (Wells 1999). It is through talk that we gain fuller understandings. This point is taken up in the next section, on reflective practice as dialogue.

6.3.2 Reflective practice as dialogue

Two of the 'problems' of reflective practice outlined above are that it is often conducted in a written form and that it is often an individual enterprise – neither of these formats, we have argued, are particularly conducive to professional development (see also McCabe et al. 2011). Any revitalisation of RP, I suggest, should promote dialogic collaboration. Understanding experiential knowledge entails collaborative discussion where thoughts and ideas about classroom practice are first articulated and then reformulated in a progression towards enhanced understanding. Reflection on practice does not occur in isolation, but in discussion with another practitioner, a form of cooperative development, involving a 'Speaker' and an 'Understander', who enhances professional understanding through dialogue (cf. Edge

2001). This position is strengthened when we consider the position of social views of learning such as those advocated under sociocultural theory. Here, the position is clear: all human development is underpinned by language, often talk (cf. Vygotsky 1978). Quite simply, if we wish to develop, understand or improve in any aspect of our lives, one of the first steps is to talk about it. New ideas are first discussed with another professional and then 'appropriated', whereby we gain ownership. The importance of this dialogic approach to teacher development is evidenced in the data extracts which follow.

In extract 6.4, two teachers are looking at their verbal behaviour and discussing their use of 'teacher echo' (repetitions) in an ESL context involving a group of multilingual adult learners:

Extract 6.4

T1: I was struck by how much echoing I did before and sometimes there was a justification for it … but a LOT of the time … it was just echo for the sake of echo so I was fairly consciously trying NOT to echo this time.

T2: And what effect did that (**reduced echo**) have on the interaction patterns or the involvement of learners in the class, did it have any effect that you noticed?

T1: I think that it made them more confident perhaps in giving me words because it was only going to come back to them if the pronunciation WASn't right rather than just getting ((1)) straight back to them. When you're eliciting vocabulary if they're coming out with the vocabulary and it's adequate and it's clear, there's no need for you to echo it back to the other students … you're wasting a lot of time by echoing stuff back.

In this extract, T1 is reflecting on her use of 'echo', the repetition of student contributions – a common feature of classroom discourse. Her realisation that echo can become a kind of habit ('echo for echo's sake') is probed by T2 who asks about the effect of echo on learner involvement. T1's response is quite revealing: she says that reduced echo makes learners more confident and that a lot of echo is unnecessary. Her self-awareness and ability to evaluate her use of one teaching practice (echo) may not have occurred without an opportunity to discuss echo and reflect on its effects. T2's question allows her to think about her language use and give reasons, possibly for the first time. It is this kind of 'light bulb moment' which professional dialogue can create. Through talk, new realisations and greater insights come about and get their first airing. This coincides with van Lier's ideas on ecological research: detailed understandings of small issues build up over time to enable teachers to grow and develop.

A similar feature is presented and discussed in extract 6.5 below. Here, the teacher Nick (N) is discussing 'wait-time' with a colleague Irene (I). Wait-time refers to the length of time a teacher waits after asking a question or inviting a student contribution – typically, it is less than one second. Extract 6.5 is taken from an action research project in which teachers were considering their use of language and interaction in an adult ESL setting (Walsh 2006).

Extract 6.5

N: I just found it was very enjoyable and the feedback, like extended wait-time. Lots of GAPS here where you think there's nobody replying and then they suddenly come in

I: Was that conscious or was that just something…?

N: No I deliberately because I know that the far-easterners have problems speaking and therefore I gave them I just gave them whatever time they needed you know. In some cases they're processing the question and they're processing the information and they HAVE to literally look into their own minds and do they have an experience which relates to the question. And this is the case I think particularly with Roy with Yung rather and Jang who are Korean I think the wait-time is ALways more extensive for them.

In this example of reflective practice as dialogue, we see how, for Nick, there is a growing realisation of the value of wait-time in whole class open discussion (*I just gave them whatever time they needed*). He comments on what actually happens following a teacher prompt (*they're processing the question … and they HAVE to literally look into their own minds and do they have an experience which relates to the question*) and makes the interesting observation that for some students, this takes more time and they need to be given that time (*the wait-time is ALways more extensive for them*).

It is apparent from Nick's comments that this is the first time he has been in a position to actually think about wait-time as an important phenomenon and one which teachers need to incorporate into their teaching. Arguably, a spoken rather than written form of RP and the involvement of a colleague allowed Nick to analyse this aspect of his teaching in far greater detail and make changes by increasing wait-time where necessary. Note too how his colleague, Irene, plays an important role in guiding the discussion and in helping Nick to clarify his own thinking around a particular issue.

A dialogic approach to reflective practice, I am suggesting, addresses the need for more spoken forms of reflection and for a collaborative, rather than individual, approach. Comments from participants in a previous study (McCabe et al. 2011) confirm the importance of dialogue and collaboration. Extracts 6.6 and 6.7 below are taken from focus group interviews with Canadian teacher educators.

Extract 6.6

Not only did they write it (reflections), they have to go away and read, and they themselves pick what they want to reflect on. They write it but then they come back and talk, and I think the talking part is as equally important as the writing part, and they talk with their colleagues in groups of four, and I'm always amazed, as well as the students. I think it's a real eye opener for them.

Extract 6.7

We let our students know that reflection is not something that's done always by yourself. If they can get involved in kind of a collaborative community of learners, it may work for them.

In extract 6.6, it is interesting to note that this teacher educator highlights the importance of talk in reflection (*they write it but then they come back and talk about it and I think the talking part is as equally important as the writing part*). He makes two points which are relevant to the present discussion: first, there is value in getting student-teachers to choose for themselves what they wish to discuss with colleagues (*they themselves pick what they want to reflect on*); second, the usefulness of shared reflections for professional development (*it's a real eye-opener for them*). It is clear from these comments that an individual's professional development is as closely linked to reflections made by peers as to that individual's own reflections on him- or herself.

It is also noteworthy to comment on the value of delaying discussion. In extract 6.6, for example, student-teachers first reflect, then write, then reflect again and then discuss. It is clear that 'reflection at a distance' has considerable merit, especially if students have completed an appropriate task as part of that process. The ensuing talk is likely to be richer and more considered than if trainees had been asked to discuss their reflections immediately after teaching. A further consideration is the need for appropriate tools which promote reflection – this is the focus of the next section.

6.3.3 Appropriate tools for RP

I have already commented on the nature of this problem (see above): there is presently a lack of appropriate tools for professional development, a tendency to use the same tool no matter what the stage of development, a focus on the written form, and the need for tools which are designed by and for teachers rather than by researchers. RP tools should be designed with a particular context in mind, by participants in that context and with a clear focus. Where reflective practice tools are used as part of a teacher education programme, they should vary according to the stage they are used and in response to genuine trainee needs. Tools should ideally really help teachers to engage with their professional practices and promote new levels of understanding. Linking to the previous discussion, appropriate tools should allow data collection and promote discussion.

Here, I present examples of the kinds of tool which teachers might use to collect evidence.

'Ad hoc' self-observation

In a critical review of current approaches to reflective practice, Gray and Block draw particular attention to courses that are excessively school based (programmes like CELTA and PGCE) where there is not sufficient time or opportunity for an exploratory or reflective talk that is 'facilitated by the use of theoretical tools and concepts'. They see this as part of 'a McDonaldised system designed to produce teachers capable of using basic tools of the trade such as textbooks in ways which are efficient, calculable and predictable and which guarantee the delivery of a standardised product into the educational marketplace' (2012: 114). They refer to Pennycook (1994) in making the point that 'reflective theorising practitioners are not at all what this sector requires'. Essentially, they point to a 'commodification' of English language teaching (cf. the reference to McDonalds) and a deskilling of the TESOL profession.

The criticisms raised by Gray and Block are both applauded and supported both here and elsewhere in this book. The unthinking use of checklists and pro-formas has been criticised in the earlier parts of this chapter. This said, there is a case to be made for the use of 'ad hoc' instruments, designed for specific tasks in specific contexts (cf. Wallace 1998). Such an approach permits up-close self-observation and allows for the emergence of a detailed understanding of professional practice, without the need for a transcription or recording. One example of such an instrument was devised by Walsh (2006). The SETT (self-evaluation of teacher talk) framework was designed in collaboration with a group of university TESOL teachers and used to help teachers gain closer understandings of the complex relationship between language, interaction and learning. As we saw in Chapter 4, essentially, it is a generic instrument comprising four micro-contexts (called modes) and 14 interactional features (such as clarification request, display question, teacher echo). By recording their classes and then completing the SETT grid, teachers establish a 'snapshot' of their verbal behaviour while teaching. It has been used in and adapted to a range of contexts globally and is now used on initial teacher education courses in, for example, Singapore, Ireland and Taiwan (see Walsh 2011). Similar tools have been advocated by other researchers with the overall goal of making classrooms more dialogic and more engaging for learners (see, for example, Mortimer and Scott 2003 and Alexander 2008). The use of an 'ad hoc' approach to self-observation has particular merit since it is context specific and encourages particular teaching practices to be studied in some detail.

In extract 6.8 below, the teacher, Joy, has analysed her teaching using the SETT framework and is talking about her evaluation with a colleague, Mike. The focus of the reflection is scaffolding.

Extract 6.8

Mike: Is scaffolding something you think you do more of in that type of mode for example you're in a skills and systems mode here. Do you think it's something that happens more in some modes than others or is it maybe too difficult to say at this stage?

Joy: My first feeling would be yes because it's so focused on language that anything they give me that might not be correct and not clear then I'm going to re-formulate it or anything they don't understand I'm going to give them a lot of examples so that's all scaffolding isn't it?

Joy's comments indicate that she is trying to both understand for herself and explain to Mike how scaffolding occurs in practice (*I'm going to re-formulate it ... I'm going to give them a lot of examples so that's all scaffolding isn't it?*). Joy explains that scaffolding occurs more in skills and systems mode because this is the mode where the main focus is the language itself (*it's so focused on language*). Mike plays a key role in this extract in helping Joy to clarify her own reflections and understand when a particular practice occurs and explain why (cf. Edge 2001). Essentially, he plays the role of a neutral observer; with no particular agenda, he is able to simply act as a sounding board for Joy, questioning and helping her to clarify her thinking.

Evidenced here is a process of reflection through dialogue, a more effective means of encouraging engaged RP and clarifying misunderstandings. Here, Joy clarifies her understanding of scaffolding and gives reasons for doing it. Through talk, new realisations and greater insights come about and get their first airing. Dialogue can establish 'proximal processes', or contexts that create opportunities for learning potential, which, according to Bronfenbrenner and Ceci (1994: 578), offer development growth in terms of:

- Differentiated perception and response.
- Directing and controlling one's own behaviour.
- Coping successfully under stress.
- Acquiring knowledge and skill.

Modifying and constructing one's own physical, social and symbolic environment. In extract 6.8, the proximal processes established by this dialogue (accompanied by prior reflection) have enabled Joy to articulate two essential features of scaffolding: the use of examples and the use of reformulation. It is, arguably, unlikely that this degree of understanding would have occurred without the dialogue with Mike.

A second and very powerful tool which could be used to accompany dialogue is stimulated recall.

Stimulated recall

One of the most powerful means of promoting reflective practice is to get teachers to make a video or audio recording of their teaching and then discuss it with a critical friend or colleague. This procedure, known as *stimulated recall* (see, for example, Lyle 2003), has the immediate advantage of allowing both parties to watch or listen to a segment of teaching and comment on it together. It is an excellent means of raising awareness about specific features of a teacher's professional practice. In its purest form, it is used to get practitioners to actually recall specific incidents and comment on them, but it can also be used as a stimulus to provide 'talking points' and promote discussion.

In extract 6.9 below, for example, the teacher Mary is explaining how she clarified a piece of vocabulary which had been elicited. (The classroom interaction is presented on the left, the teacher's commentary on the right.)

Extract 6.9
(The teacher is eliciting vocab items
and collecting them on the board.
Learner 1 is trying to explain a word)

1 L1: discographics=

2 T: =ooh what do you mean?

3 L1: the people who not the people the
   (4) the business about music record
   series and=

4 T: =is this a word you're thinking of in
   Basque or Spanish in English I don't
   know this word 'disco-graphics' what I
   would say is er (writes on board) like
   you said 'the music business'=

5 L1: =the music business? what is the
   name of of er industry?=

6 T: =the music industry as well it's
   actually better

I was going to say it's a false friend
but I decided not to because I thought
that might confuse her ... maybe I
misunderstood her now when I look
back at it ... I understood at the time
that she meant that this was a
particular industry but maybe she
meant a business ... but I wasn't
prepared to spend a long time on that
because it didn't seem important
even though there was still a doubt
in my mind...

The classroom interaction opens with L1 contributing an 'invented' piece of vocabulary, 'discographics', which is immediately met with surprise by Mary in 2 who asks for clarification. In 3, L1 attempts an explanation and encounters some perturbation, indicated by self-initiated self-repair, a 4-second pause and word search. This is ignored by Mary in the first instance, but in 4 she interrupts (as indicated by the latched turn =). Here, Mary offers an acknowledgement of L1's previous contribution ('like you said') and then scaffolds a more 'precise' term, offering 'the music business' as a more appropriate phrase for 'discographics'. In 5, it is apparent that L1 is not satisfied with this attempted clarification, as indicated by her two questions, both suggesting some doubt and confusion, while in 6, Mary again interrupts, possibly preventing a fuller explanation from L1 and possibly causing further confusion.

On the right hand side of extract 6.9, we see Mary's own self-reflections on her own data. Her insights offer a detailed analysis of a repair strategy which may have backfired and caused more confusion. She is able to rationalise the whole process and take stock of the different courses of action taken, and alternatives rejected (*I was going to say it's a false friend but I decided not to because I thought that might confuse her*). Mary is also able to accept that she may not have understood L1's explanation and that she possibly could have allowed more time, further evidence of the interruption mentioned above. By her own admission, and as evidenced in 5 (see above), there was some uncertainty about the outcome of this repair being successfully achieved. There is doubt both in Mary's comments (*there was still a doubt in my mind*), and in the questions asked by L1 (*the music business? what is the name of industry?*).

In a second stimulated recall extract, 6.10, we see the teacher, Jo, working with a group of adult learners and eliciting information about various pop stars.

Extract 6.10
(Teacher stops the activity)

T: so you can help me because I don't know
some of these people er who's that who's that
person in picture A?

*I'm asking referential questions
here because I didn't really know
the answer to some of these. They
just told me. These are genuine
questions.*

L: Mei Chung
T: Mei Chung. What does she do?
L: she's a pop singer=
T: =she's a a pop singer … from?
L: from Taiwan=
T: =Taiwan is she famous in lots of countries?
L: I think Taiwan and Hong Kong=
T: =uh uh and in Malaysia too?
L: yes

As Jo's own comments reflect, he is asking genuine or referential questions here in which there is a real exchange of information. As we can see from the interaction, in many respects the extract resembles casual conversation. Turn-taking is rapid (indicated by latching =) and there are requests for clarification (e.g., *from?*) and acknowledgement tokens (*uh uh*). It is not immediately evident who the teacher is: this could be two friends chatting and roles are pretty symmetrical. Perhaps one of the things Jo could have mentioned in his commentary is the fact that there are opportunities here for extending learner contributions and for eliciting further information. We might even argue that learning opportunities, in the form of speaking practice, have been missed in this short extract. Nonetheless, what this and other extracts show quite clearly is the relationship between classroom interaction and teachers' comments on it; this kind of data is both highly revealing and highly suited to the promotion of reflective practice.

It is clear, from both extracts, that stimulated recall is a potentially very powerful approach which has much to offer reflective practice, offering as it does an opportunity for teachers to use data to inform their reflections and then engage in dialogue to fine tune their thinking. Even without the transcripts, much can be learned by participants and it is a methodology that brings together very nicely the various elements which, we have argued, are necessary for RP to work effectively: tools, data and dialogue. Stimulated recall is relatively easy to organise, is inexpensive and unobtrusive; yet its potential for influencing professional development is enormous.

TASK 6.3

Look at the extract below, again taken from a stimulated recall interview. What insights into this teacher's practices do we get? How do these comments inform our understanding of *classroom interactional competence*?

For 10–15 minutes, students prepare the task and check with the teacher the vocabulary they need to complete the activity. Extended wait-time is quite noticeable.	*I think you have to give them time to read it to try to figure it out for themselves and then give them the kind of space that they know that if they can't figure it out for themselves they can ask you. I think if you don't do that, they sort of frantically scrabble through everything and hope somebody else will ask and I think you do have to give them time.*

Other tools for promoting RP

In the remainder of this section, I outline a number of alternative practices which might be used to generate data and promote dialogue as part of the RP cycle. Elsewhere in this book, I have discussed the value of 'snapshot' recordings – short recordings of different lesson segments. This could be a fruitful means of collecting data, especially if it is repeated over time, with each recording having a different focus. The recording itself could then form the basis of a discussion with a colleague or critical friend.

While the main drawbacks of written reflections have been highlighted in this chapter, narrative approaches to RP are to be encouraged, especially if they include some kind of short transcription as further evidence of a particular teaching segment. Again, a narrative account may focus on a short piece of teaching and may simply describe what happened and include self-reflections on the various events which make up a lesson. This account could form the basis of a discussion in a teacher group, where accounts are compared and discussed with colleagues.

Peer observation is a potentially very useful means of promoting professional development, especially when it is organised around a particular theme or topic. Ideally, three teachers should take part and identify one issue which becomes the focus of the reflection. One teacher teachers, two observe and this is then discussed and repeated until all three teachers have done some teaching. Involving three people and making the whole reflection thematic has the advantage of removing subjectivity and making the experience less polarised. The absence of a theme makes it all too easy to compare examples of 'good' teaching and may have a negative impact on one or more teachers. Peer observation is a very useful means of promoting dialogic and evidence-based reflection.

The use of published video-recorded materials, which may have accompanying transcripts, is one way of promoting RP, while at the same time removing the 'threat' of being observed by peers. There are many excellent published video-taped materials now available; one of the best is the International House series (Carr 2006), which includes studio-quality recordings and accompanying course-book material, which also has reflective tasks. There can be great value in using this kind of material to promote discussion and debate and to encourage participants to relate the comments to their own professional practice. Again, this works well when it is incorporated in a professional body such as a teachers' group.

6.4 SUMMARY

The aim of this chapter was to revisit the construct reflective practice in an evaluation which argues that the notion of RP is tired, overused and lacks any real meaning or significance for many professionals. In many contexts, RP simply isn't working and has become outdated. At the same time, the value and importance of RP have been recognised and there is a clear and pressing need to revisit and revitalise RP in order to ensure that it continues to influence professional practice.

A number of problems with RP were identified, including the fact that it is seen by many as an institutional requirement, rather than as a procedure to enhance professional practice. I was also, like others, critical of the over-dependence on a written form of RP, especially when this is repeated and always follows the same format. I argued that RP needs to be data-led and evidence-based and that there is considerable scope for making the whole process more collaborative and dialogic.

In order to make RP a more active and engaging process, and one to which we all subscribe, I have suggested that it needs to have a clear focus. One such focus is classroom discourse; by reflecting on interactions in the classroom and by making the process of reflection itself more interactive, I have argued that we are more likely to promote fine-grained understandings of classroom practices. I have suggested that by using appropriate tools to collect evidence in the form of data, and by discussing that evidence in dialogue with another professional, there is considerable scope to promote the kind of ecological research championed by van Lier (2000). In short, my argument is that not only would reflection occur in a more active and engaged way, but the outcomes of those reflections and subsequent changes to practice would benefit learners as well.

Chapter 7

Conclusion

In the final chapter of this book the discussion focuses on the main themes which have been presented and discussed and considers what future direction each theme might take. The aim is to review the current position relating to teacher development and classroom discourse and then consider what the future might hold in terms of research and professional practice. The chapter begins with an overview of the present position of classroom discourse research.

7.1 CURRENT PERSPECTIVES ON CLASSROOM DISCOURSE

The main argument running through this book is that if we wish to improve teaching, we need to understand classroom discourse. The principal reason for studying classroom discourse is that it lies at the heart of everything that takes place in classrooms; to restate van Lier, it is 'the most important thing on the curriculum' (1996: 5). Understanding interaction helps us to understand teaching and learning and improve the ways we, as teachers, go about our professional lives. The basic premise, then, is that teacher development should pay more attention to studying classroom interaction both formally, as part of pre- and in-service teacher education programmes, and more informally, by teachers working on their own self-development. The ultimate aim of this enterprise is to improve the student experience and ensure that learning and learning opportunities are maximised (Walsh 2002).

The position taken here coincides with the one advocated by Michael Breen, quoted in full here:

> Social relationships in the classroom orchestrate what is made available for learning, how learning is done and what we achieve. These relationships and the purposeful social action of teaching and learning are directly realized through the discourse in which we participate during lessons ... Furthermore, because the data made available to learners in a classroom are a collective product with which teachers and learners must interact actively as both creators and interpreters, because what learners actually learn from the classroom is socially rather than individually constructed, any explanation of how language is learned must locate the process *within* the discourse of language lessons. (1998: 119)

The perspective on learning that Breen is proposing is clearly a social one in which learning is seen as being directly related to participation and involvement (cf. Sfard 1998; Larsen-Freeman 2010). To understand how learning occurs, we need to understand what occurs in classroom interaction, we need to know how it actually *works* and we need to develop an awareness of the highly complex relationship which prevails between interaction, language and learning. (For a fuller discussion of current debates on learning in applied linguistics, see Seedhouse et al. 2010.) The position adopted by Breen coincides very closely with the one advocated here: learning is very much a social and interactive process; consequently, learners learn best when they are actively engaged in some kind of task, activity or discussion. It is the view of learning which underpins sociocultural theories of learning and the work of scholars like Vygotsky and Lantolf. It is also a view of learning which, I have argued, underpins teacher development – teachers learn best when they are engaged in dialogue and collaboration with other professionals. We return to this below.

For more than forty years, research on classroom discourse has endeavoured to describe in some detail the main features of classroom interaction. This research has focused on the ways in which teachers modify their speech, ask questions, correct errors and maintain overall control of the interaction. A huge body of research now exists on repair (see, for example, Seedhouse 2004; Walsh 2006) and questioning (Hellermann 2008) perhaps the most commonly found features of classroom discourse in any classroom, anywhere in the world. Similarly, stemming from the work of Sinclair and Coulthard (1975), it would be fair to say that in most classrooms the IRF/E exchange structure still prevails; teachers typically ask questions, learners respond and have their responses evaluated. This is how the majority of classroom discourse is structured and this is how interaction typically advances in any educational setting. It is probably fair to say that the work of Sinclair and Coulthard has been fundamental in fostering our understanding of the very fabric of classroom discourse. As a result of their research, we understand why IRF prevails: all classroom interaction is goal-oriented and the main responsibility for setting goals lies with the teacher. More recent studies have emphasised the importance of feedback (cf. Cullen 2002) and highlight the relationship between the feedback a teacher gives and the learning which occurs. There is clearly more work to be done in this area and any future studies on classroom discourse would be well-advised to shift the focus of research away from questioning and repair towards feedback and evaluation.

More recent studies of classroom discourse have adopted a variable approach, in which the relationship between language and pedagogic goals has been investigated more closely. These studies provide us with an alternative approach to describing classroom according to specific micro-contexts or modes (see, for example, Seedhouse 2004; Walsh 2006). Rather than assuming that classroom discourse is all of a oneness, a variable approach makes the important point that language use and interaction vary according to a teacher's agenda and what is happening at a particular moment. By understanding how pedagogic goals and language use are interconnected, we obtain a different perspective on classroom discourse, and one which is more closely aligned with the decisions made by teachers and learners. Perhaps most importantly, this perspective allows us to consider how the discourse is advanced *jointly*; both teachers and learners play important roles in collectively co-constructing meanings through their interactions. An understanding of the give and take which occurs in the interaction is fundamental to understanding learning (cf. Pekarek Doehler 2010; Hellermann 2008). By understanding the interconnectedness between pedagogic goals and the language used to achieve them, much has been done to unveil how learning takes place and how language, interaction and learning are inextricably entwined (cf. Seedhouse 2004). Put simply, by developing an understanding of interaction, we are advancing our understandings of learning.

From this brief discussion, it is apparent that the main reason for studying classroom discourse has changed little in more than forty years: we study classroom discourse in order to better understand learning. The focus of description and analysis is the interaction which takes place and the rationale is to gain a closer understanding of learning as the first step towards improving teaching. What has changed, however, is the approach to investigation. Previous chapters provided an overview of some of the main approaches to the study of classroom discourse, reviewing the work which has been conducted from interaction analysis, discourse analysis and conversation analysis perspectives. Each approach has its own merits and shortcomings and should be adapted to local contexts. For example, it would be unrealistic, in most situations, for teachers to provide detailed transcripts of their classes using conversation analysis; equally, for most classroom research, interaction analysis does not provide the kind of detail needed to gain a close understanding of the interaction.

Largely owing to the developments taking place in technology, it is now possible to offer alternative approaches to the investigation of classroom discourse, using, for example, corpus linguistics. Software packages (such as *Wordsmith Tools*, Scott 1996) can scan an electronic corpus in micro seconds and provide vital information about word frequencies, collocations, key words and so on. (For applications of corpus linguistics to teaching and learning, see, for example, O'Keeffe et al. 2007.) Corpus linguistics is a powerful tool for analysing spoken discourse, especially when it is harnessed with another approach such as conversation analysis (see Chapter 5). In addition to offering insights into the interactions taking place, such a combined approach also allows us to consider how particular linguistic features are used in classroom interaction, such as discourse markers, modal verbs, pronouns and so on (see Yang 2013). In developing an understanding of classroom discourse, it is important to acknowledge that we also need to look at the interplay of both interactional and linguistic features (cf. Fung and Carter 2007). Corpus linguistics allows us to look at specific linguistic features such as vague language (words such as *like, I mean, kind of,* etc.), which play a key role in creating a safe learning environment and creating shared space where learning can occur (O'Keeffe et al. 2007).

Of growing interest in recent years is the work on interactional competence (see, for example Kelly Hall et al. 2011). These studies offer new insights into the ways in which learners accomplish tasks and participate competently through a second language. Using micro analysis to study the finer details of interactions across a range of contexts, this body of research has contributed enormously to our understandings of how different interactional and linguistic resources are deployed across a variety of practices. Research projects such as *English Profile* (see Chapter 3) are now predicting that interactional competence will become the 'fifth skill' in the future, requiring new approaches to teaching and assessment. Of paramount importance in all of this work is that there is likely to be a dramatic shift towards the position currently adopted in most classrooms towards language. Rather than being seen as an object for study, like any other school subject, language is likely to be increasingly viewed as a skill; rather than studying what language *is*, the focus will shift to what language *does* in human communication. This will have repercussions for teachers, learners, materials writers, teacher educators and examination authorities.

One development which must be mentioned in a discussion on classroom discourse is the extent to which our understanding of what constitutes a classroom has changed. In light of ongoing and rapid developments in technology, the traditional physical boundaries of the classroom no longer apply. Many teachers now work in contexts in which technology plays a considerable role; they find themselves teaching and supporting learning by means of virtual learning environments (VLEs), computer mediated communication (CMC), through the use of email, blogs, podcasts and so on. Clearly, the impact of technology in the last twenty years has been huge and is set to grow even further. These developments have to be incorporated into our understandings of interaction and of the ways in which interaction impacts on teaching and learning. Technology mediated interaction is a growing area of research and one in which new understandings will emerge over time.

To summarise this brief overview of the current position of classroom discourse, we can say that, depending on the approach taken to analysis, the basic structure of classroom discourse remains the same. Most classrooms around the world are dominated by question and answer routines which can be located within IRF routines. That said, when teaching goals and the language used to achieve them are considered together, a different perspective emerges, enabling more detailed, microscopic analysis of micro-contexts. Related to this point is the fact that interaction and learning are inextricably linked: if we wish to improve the learning that takes place, we should begin by analysing interactions between teachers and learners. This process of studying classroom discourse has been greatly facilitated by technological advances coupled with alternative approaches to studying classroom discourse. These developments have resulted in the emergence of different perspectives on the nature of classroom discourse and the relationship between interactional and linguistic features. Finally, understandings of classroom interaction have been greatly advanced by the recent body of knowledge accumulated under the notion of interactional competence.

In the next section, I present a review of the main themes explored in the book and consider how each theme might change or develop in the future.

7.2 TEACHER DEVELOPMENT: CURRENT ISSUES AND FUTURE DIRECTIONS

7.2.1 L2 teacher education and sociocultural theory

As I have shown in the previous section, the principal reason for studying classroom discourse is the very close relationship between interaction and learning. This view of learning can be extended to teacher development, where learning and professional growth occur most effectively through interactions with colleagues or 'expert knowers'. The main attraction of this perspective is that teachers collectively and actively construct their own knowledge and understanding by making connections, building mental schemata and concepts through collaborative meaning making. At the heart of this theoretical position is the fact that new understandings are *mediated* by language; issues are first identified and discussed publicly and then internalised privately as teachers gain ownership. Using the words of Lantolf, we can say that although thought and speech are separate, they are 'tightly interrelated in a dialectic unity in which publicly derived speech completes privately initiated thought' (2000: 7). From a teacher education perspective, we can easily extend these ideas to demonstrate how teachers first gain new knowledge, new ideas or new understandings through interacting with colleagues or educators. This 'publicly derived' new knowledge is then privately internalised as the same teachers take ownership and apply new practices to their own context. The process is both dialectic and dialogic: it entails teachers collaborating with their peers to develop new understandings which are then internalised as a personal or individual practice.

Other researchers, notably Karen Johnson (2009), have adopted a sociocultural perspective on second language teacher education. Johnson applies this theory to studying the ways in which teachers learn to teach, how teachers perceive language, how teachers teach a second language and how they regard professional development. Her work makes an invaluable contribution to our understanding of second language teacher professional development and points to the need for future research in this area. Of particular interest in the future would be studies which look at specific sociocultural constructs in a teacher education and professional development context. For example, how do teachers *appropriate* new understandings of their practices? That is, how do teachers gain ownership of a new teaching practice; in what ways are they able to revisit existing practices and extend their professional knowledge? What *affordances*, or opportunities for learning (cf. van Lier 2000), exist in a professional development context and how might teachers make use of these in their own growth? How do teacher educators *scaffold* the contributions made by trainee teachers during post-teaching feedback sessions (cf. Harris 2013). And in what ways might socio-cultural theories of learning help us to develop new understandings of teacher learning, teacher cognitions and teacher identity (cf. Morton 2012)? In short, socio-cultural theory has much to offer in terms of developing our understandings of teacher development and in maximising the potential for professional growth.

7.2.2 Teachers as researchers

One of the main arguments of this book is that teachers need to become researchers of their own practice. Essentially, this involves teachers using tools which will allow them to access, in some detail, the contexts in which they teach in order to develop fine-grained understandings of classroom processes. I have argued that for this to actually 'work' in practice, teachers should be taught how to reflect as part of their initial teacher education programme.

I argued in Chapters 2 and 5 that for teachers to become researchers of their own classes and gain up-close, detailed 'ecological' (van Lier 2000) understandings of their local context, RP needs to be revitalised and refocused (see also Mann and Walsh 2013). A refocusing of RP entails teachers using appropriate tools, data and dialogue with other professionals. There is, I suggest, a strong and pressing need for specific changes to be made on teacher education programmes so that these essential elements of reflective practice (tools, data and dialogue) are incorporated more effectively. The consequence of this would then be that teachers would become researchers of their own practice, not, as is the situation today, for the duration of the course they are taking, but for their entire career. For this to occur, there is a need for RP to be taught on pre-service teacher education programmes (cf. Russell 2005). I would go further and argue the need for a 'third strand' in second language teacher education curricula. This strand, called something like 'interactional competence' would complement existing strands such as teaching methodology and subject knowledge by making classroom interaction the focus of study. By reflecting on interaction, I have argued, teachers will be better able to research their own practices.

In addition to teachers being taught how to reflect on their practices, I propose that they should be given appropriate tools to facilitate reflection and recognise that RP should be evidence-based using data taken from their classrooms. A challenge for the future, then, is to devise appropriate tools to collect evidence (see below) and to consider alternative forms of data. One of the arguments presented in Chapter 5 is that many of the instruments currently used on teacher education programmes are designed with the institution in mind not the individual trainee teacher (cf. Gray and Block 2012). Appropriate tools are ones which are fit for purpose (Cohen et al. 2011) and which are designed with a specific context in mind. Similarly, data means anything which helps to promote understanding; while recordings are useful, there are other types of evidence which might be equally valuable such as peer observation, feedback from students, minute papers and so on. Essentially, for teachers to become researchers, they need to learn to 'read' their environment (cf. van Lier 2000) by using whatever evidence they are able to.

7.2.3 Approaches to the study of classroom discourse

A key element in promoting understandings of classroom discourse is the approach taken to study. Different research methodologies give different perspectives and high-light certain features of the interaction. The work of Firth and Wagner (1997, 2007) has been instrumental in promoting much greater sensitivity towards contextual and interactional aspects of language use by focusing more on the participants in SLA research and less on cognitive processes. Since the late 1990s, these studies have highlighted the ways in which learning and interactional competence can be approached and described through a micro-analytic mode of inquiry (see, for example, Hellermann 2008; Markee 2008; Pekarek Doehler 2010). From this body of research has emerged the field now known as CA-SLA or CA-for-SLA: Conversation Analysis for Second Language Acquisition. By focusing on micro-details of video- or audio-recorded interaction, CA-for-SLA aims to document micro-moments of learning and understanding by drawing upon participants' own understanding of the ongoing interaction, from an emic perspective. This perspective is revealed through a detailed analysis of vocal (words and grammar, suprasegmentals, pace of talk, etc.) and non-vocal (silence, body language, embodiment of surrounding artefacts, etc.) resources within the sequential development of talk. CA-for-SLA studies have succeeded in demonstrating 'good' examples of 'interactional competence' and/or understanding of certain information by students by using interactionally and pedagogically fruitful instances of talk; for instance through the use of repair sequences (e.g., Hellermann 2009; 2011).

In terms of describing classroom discourse, there is no doubt that the use of CA has much to offer. The main aim is to account for the structural organisation of the interaction as determined by the participants; the data are allowed to 'speak for themselves' and there is no attempt to 'fit' the data to preconceived categories. The approach, then, is strictly empirical. CA also recognises that any context is not static and fixed, but dynamic and variable; contexts are not fixed entities which operate across a lesson, but dynamic and changing processes which vary from one stage of a lesson to another (Cullen 1998). A CA methodology is better equipped to take variations in linguistic and pedagogic purpose into account since one contribution is dependent on another. Finally, CA offers a multi-layered perspective on classroom discourse. Because no one utterance is categorised in isolation and because contributions are examined in sequence, a CA methodology is much better equipped to interpret and account for the multi-layered structure of classroom interaction. In short, CA has the greatest potential to account for what 'really happens' and offers the kind of detail needed to make sense of the complexity of classroom interaction.

From a research perspective, future challenges in the study of classroom discourse will be concerned with collecting data which offers greater insights into what really happens in classrooms. Current, and likely future, developments have seen CA being combined with other methodologies such as corpus linguistics (see for example Walsh et al. 2010). There is, increasingly, a likelihood that CA will become more quantitative and use larger corpora. It is also quite possible that advances in technology will permit the quantification of certain features of discourse such as turn-openers and discourse markers (see Yang 2013). Multiple method research is likely to play an important part in helping researchers uncover what is going on in language classrooms. In addition to using technology, another aspect of this is to involve participants more in the analysis. So many corpus-based studies do not interview participants – this is surely essential if we are to maximise our understanding of classroom interaction.

Note that while I am advocating some form of CA for the description of classroom discourse, I am not suggesting that teachers should use it in their own professional development. It is far too time-consuming and would take years to attain any level of proficiency. I am, however, proposing that teachers do need appropriate tools at their disposal, discussed under the next theme.

7.2.4 Appropriate tools

One of the central arguments of this book has been that teachers' professional development should be data led; if teachers are to improve their practice, I suggest, they need to collect evidence (see above). While recordings are perhaps one of the best kinds of evidence, it would be unrealistic to expect teachers to spend hours transcribing and analysing their data. By using an appropriate tool, such as an *ad hoc* instrument like the SETT framework, I have tried to offer alternative approaches to collecting and analysing data, though it is also apparent that there is still much to be done in helping teachers to access usable data (see below). Essentially, the SETT framework is intended to enable teachers to gain close, detailed understandings of their local context. While it may need to be adapted to that context, it permits a dynamic analysis of L2 classroom discourse by paying close attention to intentions and events.

In earlier chapters I suggested that the aim of recording teachers' classes is to provide a 'snapshot' – 10 to 15 minutes of one stage of the lesson. Most teachers are concerned to develop their professional expertise and make sure that their learners have a rewarding and enjoyable experience. Analysing short recordings using some kind of tool or framework, preferably developed by teachers for their own use, is a much more realistic goal than wholesale transcription of a full lesson. The aim should be to collect small amounts of data from a sample of lessons and build up a profile of a teacher's classroom interactional competence. From this, changes to practice can be made and evaluated over time.

There is a clear and pressing need for the development of tools by and for teachers to help them develop understandings of their local context. Although there are many self-observation instruments available, they are often too generic and do not promote detailed understanding. A possible way forward is for teachers to be given guidance, during their teacher education programme, on collecting and using class-based data. This might entail instruction on designing self-observation instruments or analysing video-recorded material as a means of increasing awareness of interactional processes. Whatever approach is adopted, the first steps should be sensitisation and awareness-raising, before moving on to actual data collection. Again, it is highly likely that technology will play a key role in awareness-raising; using interactive media such as Skype and blogs enables teachers to share their concerns and issues and discuss them more openly.

7.2.5 CIC and teacher development

As mentioned previously, interactional competence, the 'fifth skill', is set to become one of the major influences on language teaching, testing and materials design. Previous studies recognise that both interactional competence and CIC (classroom interactional competence) are highly context specific (see for example Young 2008; Markee 2008). In Chapter 3, a full and detailed description of some of the features of CIC was presented. While CIC is context specific, certain features were found to occur across all contexts. These include the need for pedagogic goals and language use to coincide (cf. Seedhouse 2004); the ways in which space for learning can be created or closed down through a teacher's use of language and interactional resources (Walsh and Li 2013); the extent to which teachers are able to 'shape' learner contributions by reformulating, paraphrasing and so on.

The teaching practices and interactional competencies which make up CIC vary across contexts, even within one lesson, when a variable approach to the study of discourse is adopted. One of the challenges for teacher development in the future is to characterise CIC across a range of contexts. It would be unrealistic to adopt a 'one size fits all' approach to this. Understanding what constitutes 'competence' in one context is related to a detailed understanding of that context. This will entail collecting and analysing classroom data and using appropriate tools to analyse the data. Such an opportunity provides an opening for teachers to become researchers of their own practice and to enhance understandings of their own professional practice. In short, it presents teachers with an occasion to engage in research which will ultimately benefit themselves and their learners, as opposed to 'having research done to them' by outside researchers.

There are sure to be many other future directions that classroom discourse research might take. What is clear is that there has to be a continuation of the current trend of involving practitioners and ensuring that they both benefit from new advances in knowledge and play a key role in producing that new knowledge. The challenge for the future is to get teachers involved in studying and learning about the context in which they teach by becoming researchers of that context. Teacher development is, and always will be, concerned with the endless search for improvements to professional practice; those improvements are likely to occur more quickly and last longer once teachers have acquired a fine-grained understanding of their local context.

Commentaries on Tasks

Chapter 2

TASK 2.1

A

The issue here is the students' understanding of 'might'. They interpret it in a literal sense, whereby they have a choice: either they do the exercise or they don't. In fact, the teacher's intended meaning was for the students to do the exercise. She was giving an order rather than offering a choice.

B

Here, the child, either accidentally or deliberately, is flouting the normal 'maxims' of conversation (cf. Grice). The father's intended meaning is 'say hello to Grandma'; this has been interpreted by the child as a question rather than a request and she politely says 'no'. Note how she uses the same degree of politeness as her father in her response.

C

Again, we see what happens when the normal rules of conversation are broken. Here, in the last turn, the employee gives a rather direct, even rude, response, prompted by the commuter's dispreferred response (well there's nothing nearby) and request for further help (what should I do?).

TASK 2.2

The main focus of this interaction is group discussion, and the teacher's aim is to elicit attitudes and feelings, prompted by her elicitation in line 11. However, the error in line 12 prompts the teacher's correction in line 13. It is an extended repair which, arguably, redirects the interaction towards a focus on grammar rather than discussion. A more direct repair strategy might have been more appropriate, or the error could have been ignored completely. The consequence of a teacher 'jumping in' in this way during open class discussion is often to re-direct the interaction towards form-focused activity and away from a more fluency focused activity.

Chapter 3

TASK 3.1

The response to this question is very much dependent on your own context: the age and level of your students, their previous experience of learning a language, preferred learning orientation and so on. In order to answer the question, then, focus on the skills and competencies that teachers and learners need to acquire to work together. Practices such as avoiding interruptions, seeking extended learner contributions, minimising repair during certain classroom activities, listening and responding to learner contributions and so on will almost certainly be important in any context. Spend a little time self-observing next time you teach. Which practices might be described under interactional competence; which ones would you like to develop and which might you prefer to avoid?

TASK 3.2

Extract 3.5(a)
Features of CIC:

- The teacher's use of signposting to mark the beginning and end of an activity (e.g., *okay, let's move on*).
- The teacher's modelling of key language items such as *when's your birthday?*
- Locating learning in time and space: *there are two questions on the board.*
- Direct repair in line 18 (of May) which has minimal interruption.
- Prompting in line 20: *money, books.*
- Students' ability to 'recognise the cues', make appropriate responses.
- Students' ability to maintain the flow and minimise pauses, overlaps, etc.
- There is minimal trouble in this extract and it flows well because students and teacher attend to their contributions and listen carefully.

Extract 3.5(b)
Features of CIC:

- Teacher's use of signposting and gesture to make herself understood (in lines 1–3).
- Extensive use of pausing throughout, allowing students time to think and compose a response.
- Teacher's seeking clarification and 'pushing' learners for longer responses.
- Students' ability to recognise the cues and give shorter or longer responses.
- Students' ability to reformulate and offer extended responses.
- Student's ability to maintain the flow and avoid breakdowns, etc.

TASK 3.3

Any definition of CIC is highly context specific and will include both interactional and linguistic resources. You might think about the typical features of classroom discourse in any context and then try to evaluate them; these might include, for example, questioning, error correction, explaining, eliciting, the use of feedback.

In Chapter 4, I present a more detailed description of these practices, so it might be useful to read this chapter if you have no ideas.

TASK 3.4

Stimulated recall involves watching a video clip of your teaching or listening to an audio recording and then discussing it with a colleague. The main advantage is that you get to respond to your own classroom practices as they occur, allowing you more time to evaluate and think of alternative ways of conducting a class. It is a very useful procedure, especially when it is practised with a 'critical friend' such as a trusted colleague.

In this extract (3.6), we can see how the teacher shows great awareness of the need to give students space so that they can ask questions and of the importance of taking a 'back seat': allowing learners more interactional space and monitoring at a distance. Her comments (on the right) and the classroom interaction (on the left) are very much aligned in that she is able to articulate her practices very clearly; not only can she describe what happened in her class, she is able to offer reasons.

Chapter 4

TASK 4.1

When we consider any educational context, it is immediately obvious that some features are relatively fixed, in that we have little or no control over them, while others are more within our control. For example, for most teachers, the curriculum and testing procedures are fixed, while choice of materials or types of task may be more flexible.

Here, we are concerned to develop a detailed understanding of context in the unfolding interaction of a class. Contexts do not just 'happen'; they are created by teachers and learners through the co-construction of meaning, which arises in the talk of the classroom. In order to develop these 'microscopic understandings', we need to become sensitive to the ways in which we, for example, ask questions, respond to learners, deal with feedback, etc. This view of contexts is much more realistic since it recognises the ways in which contexts are created, maintained and developed through the discourse.

TASK 4.2

The modes which can be identified are:

Materials mode (lines 29–46). Here, the teacher is working closely with the course-book unit on 'Pot-luck suppers' and the interaction is tightly controlled, focusing mainly on the material and eliciting responses. Note how the discourse marker 'right' is used to direct attention to the book in line 32; this is followed with a series of IRF routines, where she elicits the various items that people might bring to this event.

Classroom context mode (lines 47–61). The switch to classroom context mode is brought about through the use of personalisation and by involving the students in an imaginary pot-luck supper. This results in an extended student turn in line 52.

Skills and systems mode (lines 62–70). The switch to skills and systems occurs in line 62 with the introduction of the new vocabulary item 'fussy'. This is a rather abrupt switch and might potentially have resulted in some kind of breakdown. The remainder of the extract is tightly controlled and the teacher regains control of the discourse which reverts to a more traditional IRF sequence.

Chapter 5

TASK 5.1
Recording any classroom interaction is notoriously difficult. The main issue is that we are dealing with multi-party talk and it is difficult or even impossible to capture everything on a recording. Problems include not being able to hear what was said, missing key gestures or asides, capturing overlapping speech, not being able to account for certain events or episodes (some of which may have a 'history'). Deciding where to position equipment is key to this: for video recordings, we need one camera at the front and one at the back, accompanied by portable recorders positioned around the room if possible. Using lapel microphones maybe also help to capture as much of the detail as possible, while the use of field notes to describe what happened is also useful.

TASK 5.2
The approach to data collection and analysis is very much dependent on how much detail you need and what you plan to use the data for. If you need to capture as much of the detail as possible, you may decide to transcribe everything and use conversation analysis to make sense of the data. This is immensely time-consuming and may not be necessary if you're only interested in certain features of the discourse. Alternatively, you may decide to opt for 'snapshot' recordings (short 10–15 minutes each) which focus on one incident or episode or one feature of the discourse. You may decide that transcription is not necessary and use some kind of framework to capture the interaction (see Chapter 4).

Chapter 6

TASK 6.1
Reflective practice entails thinking about your professional experiences, focusing on one or two issues or 'puzzles', collecting some kind of evidence or data to illustrate the nature of the issue, and then making changes to your practice. It is probably best done with a colleague or critical friend, and dialogue is central to understanding. You may want to evaluate the change to practice in order to assess its impact on your teaching. Most of us reflect on our practice some of the time and it may be more intuitive than systematic.

TASK 6.2

The questions you write will obviously depend on your context and on the changes you'd like to make to your practice. The key issue here is ensuring that the questions you propose are answerable and that they are evidence-based. In other words, you need to select questions which require you to collect data, analyse that data, and use the analysis in any future changes to practice. By data, I mean anything which can inform your decision-making: a recording, a conversation with students, a peer observation, a piece of material, a task, a test result. Questions need to be SMART:

Systematic
Measureable
Achievable
Realistic
Timely

TASK 6.3

These comments highlight the value of allowing students 'space for learning' (see, for example, Walsh and Li 2013); that is, the kind of space where they can try things out, make mistakes, struggle, ask each other for help and, if necessary, seek advice from the teacher. Allowing space is central to maximising learning and learning opportunity. Increasing wait-time, providing time for rehearsal, and encouraging students to refine their contributions are all ways in which this kind of space can be maximised and optimised. Note that this is not the same thing at all as simply handing over to learners and letting them 'get on with it'; the teacher still plays an important role and can be called upon at any time to offer support and guidance.

Transcription System

T:	–	teacher
L:	–	learner (not identified)
L1: L2: etc.	–	identified learner
LL:	–	several learners at once or the whole class
/ok/ok/ok/	–	overlapping or simultaneous utterances by more than one learner
[do you understand?] [I see]	–	overlap between teacher and learner
=	–	turn continues, or one turn follows another without any pause (latching).
(.)	–	pause of one second or less
(4)	–	silence; length given in seconds
((4))	–	a stretch of unintelligible speech with the length given in seconds
::		A colon after a vowel or a word is used to show that the sound is extended. The number of colons shows the length of the extension.
(hm, hh)		These are onomatopoetic representations of the audible exhalation of air.
.hh		This indicates an audible inhalation of air, for example, as a gasp. The more h's, the longer the in-breath.

?	A question mark indicates that there is slightly rising intonation.
.	A period indicates that there is slightly falling intonation.
,	A comma indicates a continuation of tone.
–	A dash indicates an abrupt cut off, where the speaker stopped speaking suddenly.
↑↓	Up or down arrows are used to indicate that there is sharply rising or falling intonation. The arrow is placed just before the syllable in which the change in intonation occurs.
Under	Underlines indicate speaker emphasis on the underlined portion of the word.
CAPS	Capital letters indicate that the speaker spoke the capitalised portion of the utterance at a higher volume than the speaker's normal volume.
°	This indicates an utterance that is much softer than the normal speech of the speaker. This symbol will appear at the beginning and at the end of the utterance in question.
> <, < >	'Greater than' and 'less than' signs indicate that the talk they surround was noticeably faster, or slower, than the surrounding talk.
(would)	When a word appears in parentheses, it indicates that the transcriber has guessed as to what was said, because it was indecipherable on the tape. If the transcriber was unable to guess as to what was said, nothing appears within the parentheses.
T organises group	– editor's comments (in bold type)

References

Ädel, A. (2010), 'How to use corpus linguistics in the study of political discourse', in A. O'Keeffe and M. J. McCarthy (eds), *The Routledge Handbook of Corpus Linguistics*, London: Routledge, pp. 591–604.

Ahmed, M. K. (1994), 'Speaking as cognitive regulation: a Vygotskian perspective on dialogic communication', in J. P. Lantolf (ed.), *Vygotskian Approaches to Second Language Research*, Norwood, NJ: Ablex.

Akbari, R. (2007), 'Reflections on reflection: a critical appraisal of reflective practices in L2 teacher education', *System* 35(2), 192–207.

Alexander, R. J. (2008), *Towards Dialogic Teaching: Rethinking Classroom Talk* (fourth edition), York: Dialogos.

Alger, C. (2006), '"What went well, what didn't go so well": growth of reflection in pre-service teachers', *Reflective Practice* 7, 287–301.

Allen, J. P. B., M. Froehlich and N. Spada (1984), 'The communicative orientation of language teaching: an observation scheme', in J. Handscombe, R. Orem and B. P. Taylor (eds), *On TESOL 83: The Question of Control*, Washington, DC: TESOL.

Allwright, R. L. (1984), 'The importance of interaction in classroom language learning', *Applied Linguistics* 5, 156–71.

Allwright, R. and K. Bailey (1991), *Focus on the Language Classroom: An Introduction to Classroom Research for Language Teachers*, Cambridge: Cambridge University Press.

Allwright, R. L. and R. Lenzuen (1997), 'Exploratory practice: work at the Cultura Inglesa, Rio de Janeiro, Brazil', *Language Teaching Research* 1(1), 73–9.

Bailey, K. (1996), 'The best laid plans: teachers' in-class decisions to depart from their lesson-plans', in K. M. Bailey and D. Nunan (eds), *Voices from the Language Classroom*, Cambridge: Cambridge University Press.

Bailey, K. M. and D. Nunan (eds) (1996), *Voices from the Language Classroom*, Cambridge: Cambridge University Press.

Bartlett, L. (1990), 'Teacher development through reflective teaching', in J. C. Richards and D. Nunan (eds), *Second Language Teacher Education*, Cambridge: Cambridge University Press.

Bax, S. (2003), 'The end of ELT: a context-based approach to language teaching', *English Language Teaching Journal* 53, 278–89.

Biber, D., S. Conrad and R. Reppen (1998), *Corpus Linguistics: Investigating Language Structure and Use*, Cambridge: Cambridge University Press.

Blake, R. J. (2007), 'New trends in using technology in the language curriculum', *Annual Review of Applied Linguistics* 27, 76–97.

Block, D. (1996), 'A window on the classroom: classroom events viewed from different angles', in K. M. Bailey and D. Nunan (eds), *Voices from the Language Classroom*, Cambridge: Cambridge University Press.

Borg, M. (2002), *Learning to Teach: CELTA trainees' beliefs, experiences and reflections*, PhD dissertation, University of Leeds, UK.

Boud, D., R. Keogh and D. Walker (1985), 'What is reflection in learning?', in D. Boud, R. Keogh and D. Walker (eds), *Reflection: Turning Experience into Learning*, London: Kogan Page Ltd, pp. 7–17.

Bradbury H., N. Frost, S. Kilminster and M. Zukas (eds) (2010), *Beyond Reflective Practice: New Approaches to Professional Lifelong Learning*, Abingdon: Routledge.

Breen, M. P. (1998), 'Navigating the discourse: on what is learned in the language classroom', in W. A. Renandya and G. M. Jacobs (eds), *Learners and Language Learning. Anthology Series 39*, Singapore: SEAMO Regional Language Centre.

Brock, C. (1986), 'The effects of referential questions on ESL classroom discourse', *TESOL Quarterly* 20, 47–59.

Bronfenbrenner, U. and S. J. Ceci (1994), 'Nature-nurture reconceptualised in developmental perspective: a bioecological model', *Psychological Review* 101/4, 568–86.

Brookfield, S. D. (1997), 'Assessing critical thinking', *New Directions for Adult and Continuing Education* 75, 17–29.

Brown, J. D. and T. Rodgers (2002), *Doing Applied Linguistics Research*, Oxford: Oxford University Press.

Bruner, J. (1983), *Child's Talk*, Oxford: Oxford University Press.

Bruner, J. (1990), 'Vygotsky: a historical and conceptual perspective', in L. C. Moll (ed.), *Vygotsky and Education: Instructional Implications and Applications of Sociohistorical Psychology*, Cambridge: Cambridge University Press.

Bucholtz, M. (2007), 'Variation in transcription', *Discourse Studies* 9(6), 784–808.

Burns, A. (2005), *Teaching English from a Global Perspective*, Case studies in TESOL series, Alexandria: TESOL.

Bygate, M. (1988), *Speaking*, Oxford: Oxford University Press.

Cadorath, J. and S. Harris (1998), 'Unplanned classroom language and teacher training', *English Language Teaching Journal*, 52(3), 188–95.

Carr, D. (ed.) (2006), *Teacher Training DVD Series* (Set of fifteen DVDs). London: International House.

Carr, W. and S. Kemmis (1983), *Becoming Critical: Knowing Through Action Research*, Victoria, Australia: Deakin University Press.

Carter, R. and M. J. McCarthy (2006), *Cambridge Grammar of English. A Comprehensive Guide*, Cambridge: Cambridge University Press.

Cazden, C. B. (2001), *Classroom Discourse: The Language of Teaching and Learning*, Portsmouth: Heinemann.

Chapelle, C. A. (2001), *Computer Applications in Second Language Acquisition: Foundations for Teaching, Testing and Research*, Cambridge: Cambridge University Press.

Chaudron, C. (1988), *Second Language Classrooms: Research on Teaching and Learning*, New York: Cambridge University Press.

Clarke, M. and D. Otaky (2006), 'Reflection "on" and "in" teacher education in the United Arab Emirates' *International Journal of Educational Development* 26, 111–22.

Cohen, L., L. Manion and K. Morrison (2011), *Research Methods in Education*, London: Routledge-Falmer.

Cook, G. (1989), *Discourse*, Oxford: Oxford University Press.

Cook, V. J. (2007), 'The nature of the L2 user', in L. Roberts, A. Gurel, S. Tatar and L. Marti (eds), *EUROSLA Yearbook*, 7: 205–20.

Cotterill, J. (2010), 'How to use corpus linguistics in forensic linguistics' in A. O'Keeffe and M. J. McCarthy (eds), *The Routledge Handbook of Corpus Linguistics*, London: Routledge, pp. 578–90.

Coyle, D. (1999), *Adolescent Voices Speak Out: If only they would – if only they could. A case study. The interplay between linguistic and strategic competence in classrooms where modern languages are used.* Unpublished PhD thesis, University of Nottingham.

Cullen, R. (1998), 'Teacher talk and the classroom context', *English Language Teaching Journal* 52, 179–87.

Cullen, R. (2002), 'Supportive teacher talk: the role of the F-move', *English Language Teaching Journal* 56, 117–27.

Dewey, J. (1933), *How We Think: A Restatement of the Relation of Reflective Thinking to the Educative Process*, Boston: D. C. Heath and Company.

Doyle, W. (1986), 'Classroom organisation and management', in M. C. Wittrock (ed.), *Handbook of Research on Teaching*, third edition, New York: Macmillan.

Drew, P. (1994), 'Conversation analysis', in R. E. Asher (ed.), *The Encyclopaedia of Language and Linguistics*, Oxford: Pergamon.

Drew, P. and J. Heritage (eds) (1992), *Talk at Work: Interaction in Institutional Settings*, Cambridge: Cambridge University Press.

Edge, J. (1992), *Co-operative Development*, London: Longman.

Edge, J. (2001), *Action Research*, Alexandria, VA: TESOL Inc.

Edwards, A. and D. Westgate (1994), *Investigating Classroom Talk*, London: Falmer.

Ellis, R. (1990), *Instructed Second Language Acquisition*, Oxford: Blackwell.

Ellis, R. (1998), 'Discourse control and the acquisition-rich classroom', in W. A. Renandya and G. M. Jacobs (eds), *Learners and Language Learning. Anthology Series 39*, Singapore: SEAMO Regional Language Centre.

Ellis, R. (2000), 'Task-based research and language pedagogy', *Language Teaching Research* 49, 193–220.

Ellis, R. (2001), 'Investigating form-focused instruction', in R. Ellis (ed.), *Form Focused Instruction and Second Language Learning*, Malden, MA: Blackwell.

Eraut, M. (1995), 'Schön shock: a case for reframing-in-action?', *Teachers and Teaching: Theory and Practice* 1, 9–22.

Farr, F. (2005), *Reflecting on Reflections: A corpus-based analysis of spoken post teaching practice interactions in an English language teaching academic environment*. Unpublished PhD thesis, University of Limerick, Ireland.

Farr, F. (2011), *The Discourse of Teaching Practice Feedback: An Investigation of Spoken and Written Modes*, New York: Routledge.

Firth, A. (1996), 'The discursive accomplishment of normality: on "lingua franca" English and conversation analysis', *Journal of Pragmatics* 26, 237–59.

Firth, A. and J. Wagner (1997), 'On discourse, communication, and (some) fundamental concepts in SLA research', *Modern Language Journal* 81, 285–300.

Firth, A. and J. Wagner (2007), 'Second/foreign language learning as a social accomplishment: elaborations on a reconceptualized SLA', *Modern Language Journal* 91 (Special Focus Issue on the impact of the ideas of Firth and Wagner on SLA), 798–817.

Flanders, N.A. (1970), *Analyzing Teacher Behaviour*, Reading, MA: Addison-Wesley.

Fung, L. and R. Carter (2007), 'Discourse markers and spoken English: native and learner use in pedagogic settings', *Applied Linguistics* 28(3), 410–39.

Gee, J. P. (2005), *An Introduction to Discourse Analysis*, London: Routledge.

Gillen, J. (2000), 'Versions of Vygotsky', *British Journal of Educational Studies* 48(2): 183–98.

Glew, P. (1998), 'Verbal interaction and English second language acquisition in classroom contexts', *Issues in Educational Research* 8, 83–94.

Goffman, E. (1981), *Forms of Talk*, Oxford: Oxford University Press.

Goldenberg, C. (1992), 'Instructional conversation: promoting comprehension through discussion', *The Reading Teacher* 46, 316–26.

Gower, R., D. Phillips and S. Walters (1995), *Teaching Practice Handbook*, second edition, London: Heinemann.

Gray, J. and D. Block (2012), 'The marketisation of language teacher education and neoliberalism', in D. Block, J. Gray and M. Holborow (eds), *Neoliberalism and Applied Linguistics*, London: Routledge, pp. 114–43.

Grundy, P. (2000), *Doing Pragmatics*, New York: Oxford University Press.

Grundy, S. (1987), *Curriculum: Product or Praxis*, Lewes: Falmer.

Grushka, K., J. Hynde and R. Reynolds (2005), 'Reflecting upon reflection: theory and practice in one Australian university teacher education program', *Reflective Practice* 6(2), 239–46.

Halliday, M. A. K. (1978), *Language as a Social Semiotic: the Social Interpretation of Language and Meaning*, London: Arnold.

Hargreaves, D. H. (1984),'Teacher's questions: open, closed and half-open', *Educational Research* 26(1), 46–51.

Hargreaves, J. (2004), 'So how do you feel about that? Assessing reflective practice', *Nurse Education Today* 3, 196–201.

Harmer, J. (1999), 'Abide with me: change or decay in teacher behaviour?', *IATEFL Teacher Trainer and Teacher Development Special Interest Group Newsletter* 2, 23–7.

Harris, A. (2013), *Professionals Developing Professionalism: The interactional organisation of reflective practice in post-teaching feedback*. Unpublished PhD thesis, Newcastle University.

Harrison, I. (1996), 'Look who's talking now: listening to voices in curriculum renewal', in K. M. Bailey and D. Nunan (eds), *Voices from the Language Classroom*, Cambridge: Cambridge University Press.

Hellermann, J. (2005), 'Syntactic and prosodic practices for cohesion in series of three-part sequences in classroom talk', *Research on Language and Social Interaction* 38, 105–30.

Hellermann, J. (2008), *Social Actions for Classroom Language Learning*, Clevedon: Multilingual Matters.

Heritage, J. (1997), 'Conversational analysis and institutional talk: analyzing data', in D. Silverman (ed.), *Qualitative Research: Theory, Method and Practice*, London: Sage Publications.

Heritage, J. and D. Greatbatch (1991), 'On the institutional character of institutional talk: the case of news interviews', in D. Boden and D. H. Zimmerman (eds), *Talk and Social Structure: Studies in Ethnomethodology and Conversation Analysis*, Berkeley: University of California Press.

Hickman, M. E. (1990), 'The implications of discourse skills in Vygotsky's developmental theory', in L. C. Moll (ed.), *Vygotsky and Education: Instructional Implications and Applications of Sociohistorical Psychology*, Cambridge: Cambridge University Press.

Hobbs, V. (2007), *Examining Short-term ELT Teacher Education: An ethnographic case study of trainees' experiences*. PhD dissertation, University of Sheffield, UK.

Howard, A. (2010), 'Is there such a thing as a typical language lesson?', *Classroom Discourse* 1, 82–100.

Hymes, D. (1972), 'Models of the interaction of language and social life', in J. Gumperz and D. Hymes (eds), *Directions in Sociolinguistics: The Ethnography of Communication*, New York: Holt, Rinehart and Winston, pp. 35–71.

Hymes, D. (1996), *Ethnography, Linguistics, Narrative Inequality: Towards an Understanding of Voice*, London: Taylor and Francis.

Jarvis, J. and M. Robinson (1997), 'Analysing educational discourse: an exploratory study of teacher response and support to pupils' learning', *Applied Linguistics* 18, 212–28.

Jenks, C. J. (2009), 'Getting acquainted in Skypecasts: Aspects of social organization in online chat rooms', *International Journal of Applied Linguistics* 19(1), 26–46.

Jenks, C. J. (2011), *Transcribing Talk and Interaction: Issues in the Representation of Communication Data*, Amsterdam: John Benjamins.

Jenks, C. J. (2013), *Social Interaction and Computer Mediated Communication*, Edinburgh: Edinburgh University Press.

Johns, C. (2000), *Becoming a Reflective Practitioner: A Reflective and Holistic Approach to Clinical Nursing, Practice Development and Clinical Supervision*, Oxford: Blackwell Science.

Johnson, K. (1992), 'The instructional decisions of pre-service ESL teachers: new directions for teacher preparation programmes', in J. Flowerdew, M. Brock and S. Hsia (eds), *Perspectives on Second Language Teacher Education*, Hong Kong: City Polytechnic of Hong Kong.

Johnson, K. E. (1995), *Understanding Communication in Second Language Classrooms*, Cambridge: Cambridge University Press.

Johnson, K. E. (1999), *Understanding Language Teaching: Reasoning in Action*, Boston, MA: Heinle and Heinle.

Johnson, K. E. (2009), *Second Language Teacher Education: A Sociocultural Perspective*, New York: Routledge.

Kasper, G. (2001), 'Four perspectives on L2 pragmatic development', *Applied Linguistics* 22, 502–30.

Kasper, G. (2004), 'Participant orientations in German-conversation-for-learning', *Modern Language Journal* 88, 551–67.

Kelly Hall, J., J. Hellermann and S. Pekarek Doehler (eds) (2011), *L2 Interactional Competence and Development*, New York: Multilingual Matters.

Kemmis, M. and R. McTaggart (1992), *The Action Research Planner* (third edition), Victoria, Australia: Deakin University Press.

Killion, J. and G. Todnem (1991), 'A process for personal theory building', *Educational Leadership* 48(7), 14–16.

Koester, A. (2006), *Investigating Workplace Discourse*, London: Routledge.

Kolb, D. A. (1984), *Experiential Learning: Experience as a Source of Learning and Development*, New Jersey: Prentice Hall.

Koshik, I. (2002), 'Designedly incomplete utterances: A pedagogical practice for eliciting knowledge displays in error correction sequences', *Research on Language and Social Interaction* 35: 277–309.

Kramsch, C. (1986), 'From language proficiency to interactional competence', *Modern Language Journal* 70(4), 366–72.

Krashen, S. (1985), *The Input Hypothesis*, London: Longman.

Kumaravadivelu, B. (1999), 'Critical classroom discourse analysis', *TESOL Quarterly* 33, 453–84.

Lam, W. and J. Wong (2000), 'The effects of strategy training on developing discussion skills in an ESL classroom', *English Language Teaching Journal* 54, 245–55.

Lantolf, J. P. (2000), *Sociocultural Theory and Second Language Learning*, Oxford: Oxford University Press.

Lantolf, J. P. and G. Appel (1994), 'Theoretical framework: an introduction to Vygotskian perspectives on second language research', in J. P. Lantolf and G. Appel (eds), *Vygotskian Approaches to Second Language Research*, Norwood, NJ: Ablex.

Lantolf, J. P. and S. Thorne (2006), *Sociocultural Theory and the Genesis of Second Language Development*, Oxford: Oxford University Press.

Larsen-Freeman, D. (2010), 'Having and doing: learning from a complexity theory perspective', in P. Seedhouse, S. Walsh and C. Jenks (eds), *Reconceptualising Learning in Applied Linguistics*, London: Palgrave Macmillan.

Legutke, M. and H. Thomas (1991), *Process and Experience in the Language Classroom*, Harlow: Longman.

Leinhardt, G. and J. G. Greeno (1986), 'The Cognitive Skill of Teaching', *Journal of Educational Psychology* 78(2), 75–95.

Leont'ev, A. N. (1981), *Problems of the Development of the Mind*, Moscow: Progress.

Levinson, S. (1983), *Pragmatics*, Cambridge: Cambridge University Press.

Li, L. (2008), *EFL Teachers' Beliefs About ICT Integration in Chinese Secondary Schools*. Unpublished PhD thesis, Queen's University, Belfast.

Lin, A. (2000), 'Lively children trapped in an island of disadvantage: verbal play of Cantonese working-class schoolboys in Hong Kong', *International Journal of the Sociology of Language* 143, 63–83.

Long, M. H. (1983), 'Native speaker/non-native speaker conversation and the negotiation of meaning', *Applied Linguistics* 4, 126–41.

Long, M. H. (1996), 'The role of the linguistic environment in second language acquisition', in W. C. Ritchie and T. K. Bhatia (eds), *Handbook of Second Language Acquisition*, San Diego: Academic Press.

Lyle, J. (2003), 'Stimulated recall: a report on its use in naturalistic research', *British Educational Research Journal* 29(6), 861–78.

Lyster, R. (1998), 'Recasts, repetition and ambiguity in L2 classroom discourse', *Studies in Second Language Acquisition* 20, 51–81.

McCabe, M., S. Walsh, R. Wideman, E. Winter (2011), 'The R word in teacher education: understanding the teaching and learning of critical reflective practice', *International Electronic Journal for Leadership in Learning*.

McCarthy, M. (1992), *Vocabulary*, London: Oxford University Press.

McCarthy, M. J. (2003), 'Talking back: "small" interactional response tokens in everyday conversation', *Research on Language in Social Interaction* 36, 33–63.

McCarthy, M. J. (2005), 'Fluency and confluence: what fluent speakers do', *The Language Teacher* 29(6), 26–8.

McCarthy, M. J. and R. A. Carter (2002), 'This that and the other: Multi-word clusters in spoken English as visible patterns of interaction', *Teanga* 21, 30–52.

McCarthy, M. J. and S. Walsh (2003), 'Discourse', in D. Nunan (ed.), *Practical English Language Teaching*, San Francisco: McGraw-Hill.

Mann, S. J. (2001), 'From argument to articulation', *English Teaching Professional* 20, 57–9.

Mann, S. J. and S. Walsh (2013), 'RP or "RIP": a critical perspective on reflective practice', *International Review of Applied Linguistics*, forthcoming.

Mann, S. and S. Walsh (2011), 'Shaping reflective tools to context'. Paper presented at the *Reflection in the Round: Discourses and Practices of Reflection* at the BAAL/CUP seminar, Oxford Brookes University.

Markee, N. (2008), 'Toward a learning behavior tracking methodology for CA-for-SLA', *Applied Linguistics* 29: 404–27.

Martin, J. (1985), *Reclaiming a Conversation: The Ideal of the Educated Woman*, New Haven, CT: Yale University Press.

Maykut, P. and R. Morehouse (1994), *Beginning Qualitative Research: A Philosophic and Practical Guide*, London: Falmer Press.

Mehan, H. (1979), *Learning Lessons: Social Organization in the Classroom*, Cambridge, MA: Harvard University Press.

Mercer, N. (1994), 'Neo-Vygotskyan theory and classroom education', in B. Stierer and J. Maybin (eds), *Language, Literacy and Learning in Educational Practice*, Clevedon: Multilingual Matters/Open University.

Mercer, N. (2004), 'Sociocultural discourse analysis: analysing classroom talk as a social mode of thinking', *Journal of Applied Linguistics* 1(2), 137–68.

Mercer, N. (2010), 'The analysis of classroom talk: methods and methodologies', *British Journal of Educational Psychology* 80, 1–14.

Mezirow, J. (1991), *Transformative Dimensions of Adult Learning*, San Francisco: Jossey-Bass Inc.

Mori, J. (2004), 'Pursuit of understanding: conversation analytic account of a small-group activity in a Japanese language classroom', in R. Gardner and J. Wagner (eds), *Second Language Conversations*, London: Continuum, pp. 157–77.

Mortimer, E. and P. Scott (2003), *Meaning Making in Secondary Science Classrooms*, Oxford: Oxford University Press.

Morton, T. (2012), *Teachers' Knowledge About Language and Classroom Interaction in Content and Language Integrated Learning*. Unpublished PhD thesis, Universidad Autónoma de Madrid.

Murphy, B. (2012), '"I know I have got it in me I just need to bring it out": exploring the discourse of reflective practice in teacher education', Talk given at the University of Newcastle, February 2012.

Nassaji, H. and G. Wells (2000), 'What's the use of "triadic dialogue"?: an investigation of teacher-student interaction', *Applied Linguistics* 21, 376–406.

Ng, M. and C. Lee (1996), 'What's different about cooperative learning? And its significance in social studies teaching', *Teaching and Learning* 17, 15–23.

Nunan, D. (1987), 'Communicative language teaching: making it work', *English Language Teaching Journal*, 41, 136–45.

Nunan, D. (1989), *Understanding Language Classrooms*, Hemel Hempstead: Prentice Hall.

Nunan, D. (1991), *Language Teaching Methodology*, Hemel Hempstead: Prentice-Hall.

Nunan, D. (1996), 'Hidden voices: insiders' perspectives on classroom interaction', in K. M. Bailey and D. Nunan (eds), *Voices from the Language Classroom*, Cambridge: Cambridge University Press.

Nystrand, M. (1997), 'Dialogic instruction: when recitation become conversation', in M. Nystrand, A. Gamoran, R. Kachur and C. Prendergast (eds), *Opening Dialogue: Understanding the Dynamics of Language Learning and Teaching in the English Classroom*, New York: Teachers College Press.

O'Keeffe, A. (2006), *Investigating Media Discourse*, London: Routledge.

O'Keeffe, A. and F. Farr (2003), 'Using language corpora in language teacher education: pedagogic, linguistic and cultural insights', *TESOL Quarterly* 37(3), 389–418.

O'Keeffe, A., M. McCarthy and R. Carter (2007), *From Corpus to Classroom: Language Use and Language Teaching*, Cambridge: Cambridge University Press.

Pavlenko, A. and J. P. Lantolf (2000), 'Second language learning as participation and the (re)construction of selves', in J. P. Lantolf (ed.), *Sociocultural Theory and Second Language Learning*, Oxford: Oxford University Press.

Pekarek-Doehler, S. (2010), 'Conceptual changes and methodological challenges: on language, learning and documenting learning in conversation analytic SLA research', in P. Seedhouse, S. Walsh and C. Jenks (eds), *Reconceptualising Learning in Applied Linguistics*, London: Palgrave MacMillan.

Pennycook, A. (1994), *The Cultural Politics of English as an International Language*, Harlow: Longman Group Limited.

Pica, T. (1997), 'Second language teaching and research relationships: a North American view', *Language Teaching Research* 1, 48–72.

Porter, P. (1986), 'How learners talk to each other: input and interaction in task-centred discussions', in R. Day (ed.), *Talking to Learn: Conversation in Second Language Acquisition*, Rowley, MA: Newbury House.

Psathas, G. (1995), *Conversation Analysis*, Thousand Oaks: Sage.

Rampton, B. (1999), 'Dichotomies, difference and ritual in second language learning and teaching', *Applied Linguistics* 20, 316–40.

Richards, J. C. (1990), 'The dilemma of teacher education in second language teaching', in J. C. Richards and D. Nunan (eds), *Second Language Teacher Education*, Cambridge: Cambridge University Press.

Richards, K. (2006), '"Being the teacher": identity and classroom conversation ... a response to Sheen and O'Neill', *Applied Linguistics* 27, 135–41.

Roberts, J. (1998), *Language Teacher Education*, London: Arnold.

Röhler, L. R. and D. J. Cantlon (1996), 'Scaffolding: a powerful tool in social constructivist classrooms'. Available at <http://edeb3.educ.msu.edu./Literacy/papers/paperlr2.html> (last accessed 24 June 2005).

Rosen, L. D. (2010), *Rewired: Understanding the I-Generation and the Way They Learn*, New York: Palgrave Macmillan.

Rulon, K. and J. Creary (1986). 'Negotiation of content: teacher-fronted and small-group interaction', in R. Day (ed.), *Talking to Learn: Conversation in Second Language Acquisition*, Rowley, MA: Newbury House.

Russell, T. (2005), 'Can reflective practice be taught?', *Reflective Practice* 6(2), 199–204.

Sacks, H., E. Schegloff and G. Jefferson (1974), 'A simplest systematics for the organisation of turn-taking in conversation', *Language* 50, 696–735.

Schiffrin, D. (1994), *Approaches to Discourse*, Cambridge, MA: Blackwell Publishers.

Schmidt, R. (1993), 'Awareness and second language acquisition', *Annual Review of Applied Linguistics* 13, 206–26.

Schön, D. A. (1983), *The Reflective Practitioner: How Professionals Think in Action*, New York: Basic Books.

Schön, D. A. (1996), *Educating the Reflective Practitioner Towards a New Design of Teaching and Learning in the Professions*, San Francisco: Jossey-Bass.

Scott, M. (1996), *Wordsmith Tools*, Oxford: Oxford University Press.

Seedhouse, P. (1996), *Learning Talk: A study of the interactional organization of the L2 classroom from a CA institutional discourse perspective*. Unpublished thesis, University of York.

Seedhouse, P. (1997), 'The case of the missing "no": the relationship between pedagogy and interaction', *Language Learning* 47, 547–83.

Seedhouse, P. (2004), *The Interactional Architecture of the Second Language Classroom: A Conversational Analysis Perspective*, Oxford: Blackwell.

Seedhouse, P., S. Walsh and C. Jenks (eds) (2010), *Reconceptualising Learning in Applied Linguistics*, London: Palgrave Macmillan.

Sfard, A. (1998), 'On two metaphors for learning and the dangers of choosing just one', *Educational Researcher* 27, 4–13.

Shaw, P. A. (1996), 'Voices for improved learning: the ethnographer as co-agent of pedagogic change', in K. M. Bailey and D. Nunan (eds), *Voices from the Language Classroom*, Cambridge: Cambridge University Press.

Sinclair, J. and D. Brazil (1982), *Teacher Talk*, Oxford: Oxford University Press.

Sinclair, J. and M. Coulthard (1975), *Towards an Analysis of Discourse*, Oxford: Oxford University Press.

Slimani, A. (1989), 'The role of topicalisation in classroom language learning', *System* 17, 223–34.

Spencer-Oatey, H., and V. Žegarac (2002), 'Pragmatics', in N. Schmitt (ed.), *An Introduction to Applied Linguistics*, London: Arnold, pp. 74–91.

Spiro, J. and P. Wickens (2011), *Reflection in the Round: Discourses and Practices of Reflection*, BAAL/CUP seminar (Oxford Brookes University).

Sternberg, R. (1994), 'Answering questions and questioning answers: guiding children to intellectual excellence,' *Phi Delta Kappan* 76, 135–7.

Stubbs, M. (1983), *Discourse Analysis: The Sociolinguistic Analysis of Natural Language*, Oxford: Blackwell.

Swain, M. (1985), 'Communicative competence: some roles of comprehensible input and comprehensible output in its development', in S. Gass and C. Madden (eds), *Input in Second Language Acquisition*, Rowley, MA: Newbury House.

Swain, M. (1995), 'Three functions of output in second language learning', in G. Cook and B. Seidelhofer (eds), *Principle and Practice in Applied Linguistics: Studies in Honour of H. G. Widdowson*, Oxford: Oxford University Press.

Swain, M. (2005), 'The output hypothesis: theory and research', in E. Hinkel (ed.), *Handbook on Research in Second Language Teaching and Learning*, Mahwah, NJ: Lawrence Erlbaum.

Swain, M. and S. Lapkin (1998), 'Interaction and second language learning: two adolescent French immersion students working together', *Modern Language Journal* 83, 320–38.

ten Have, P. (2007), *Doing Conversation Analysis: A Practical Guide*, London: Sage.

Thomas, J. (1995), *Meaning in Interaction: An Introduction to Pragmatics*, Harlow: Pearson Education.

Thompson, G. (1997), 'Training teachers to ask questions', *English Language Teaching Journal* 51, 99–105.

Thornbury, S. (1996), 'Teachers research teacher talk', *English Language Teaching Journal* 50, 279–89.

Tillema, T., M. Dijst and T. Schwanen (2010), 'Face-to-face and electronic communications in maintaining social networks: The influence of geographical and relational distance and of information content', *New Media and Society* 12(6), 965–83.

Tsui, A. B. M. (1985), 'Analyzing input and interaction in second language classrooms', *RELC Journal* 16(1), 8–32.

Tsui, A. B. M. (1994), *English Conversation*, Oxford: Oxford University Press.

Tsui, A. B. M. (1996), 'Reticence and anxiety in second language learning', in K. M. Bailey and D. Nunan (eds), *Voices from the Language Classroom*, Cambridge: Cambridge University Press.

Tsui, A. B. M. (1998), 'The "unobservable" in classroom interaction', *The Language Teacher* 22, 25–6.

van Lier, L. (1988), *The Classroom and the Language Learner*, London: Longman.

van Lier, L. (1991), 'Inside the classroom: learning processes and teaching procedures', *Applied Language Learning* 2(1), 48–64.

van Lier, L. (1996), *Interaction in the Language Curriculum: Awareness, Autonomy and Authenticity*, New York: Longman.

van Lier, L. (2000), 'From input to affordance: social-interactive learning from an ecological perspective', in J. P. Lantolf (ed.), *Sociocultural Theory and Second Language Learning*, Oxford: Oxford University Press.

Vygotsky, L. S. (1978), *Mind in Society: The Development of Higher Psychological Processes*, Cambridge, MA: Harvard University Press.

Vygotsky, L. S. (1986), *Thought and Language* (new edition by A. Kozulin), Cambridge, MA: MIT.

Vygotsky, L. S. (1999), *Collected Works Volume 6*, R. Rieber and M. Hall (eds), New York: Plenum Press.

Wallace, M. (1991), *Training Foreign Language Teachers*, Cambridge: Cambridge University Press.

Wallace, M. (1998), *Action Research for Language Teachers*, Cambridge: Cambridge University Press.

Walsh, S. (2001), *Characterising Teacher Talk in the Second Language Classroom: A process model of reflective practice*. Unpublished PhD thesis, Queen's University Belfast.

Walsh, S. (2002), 'Construction or obstruction: teacher talk and learner involvement in the EFL classroom', *Language Teaching Research* 6, 3–23.

Walsh, S. (2003), 'Developing interactional awareness in the second language classroom', *Language Awareness* 12, 124–42.

Walsh, S. (2006), *Investigating Classroom Discourse*, London: Routledge.

Walsh, S. (2011), *Exploring Classroom Discourse: Language in Action*, London: Routledge.

Walsh, S. and A. O'Keeffe (2007), 'Applying CA to a modes analysis of third-level spoken academic discourse', in H. Bowles and P. Seedhouse (eds), *Conversation Analysis and Languages for Specific Purposes*, Bern: Peter Lang.

Walsh, S. and K. Lowing (2008), 'Talking to learn or learning to talk: PGCE students' development of interactional competence'. Paper presented at the British Educational Research Association Conference, Herriot Watt University, Edinburgh.

Walsh, S. and L. Li (2013), 'Conversations as space for learning', *International Journal of Applied Linguistics* (forthcoming).

Walsh, S., T. Morton and A. O'Keefe (2011), 'Analyzing university spoken interaction: a corpus linguistics/conversation analysis approach', *International Journal of Corpus Linguistics* 16(3), 326–45.

Wells, G. (1999), *Dialogic Inquiry: Towards a Sociocultural Practice and Theory of Education*, Cambridge: Cambridge University Press.

Westerman, D. (1991), 'Expert and novice teacher decision making', *Journal of Teacher Education* 42(4), 292–305.

White, J. and P. M. Lightbown (1984), 'Asking and answering in ESL classes', *The Canadian Modern Language Review* 40, 228–44.

Winter, R. (1996), 'Some principles and procedures for the conduct of action research', in

O. Zuber-Skerritt (ed.), *New Directions in Action Research*, London: Falmer.

Woods, P. (1989), *Working for Teacher Development*, Dereham: Peter Francis Publishers.

Wray, A. (2000), 'Formulaic sequences in second language teaching: principle and practice', *Applied Linguistics* 21(4), 463–89.

Wray, A. (2002), *Formulaic Language and the Lexicon*, Cambridge: Cambridge University Press.

Wu, B. (1998), 'Towards an understanding of the dynamic process of L2 classroom interaction', *System* 26, 525–40.

Wu, K. Y. (1991), 'Classroom interaction and teacher questions revisited'. Unpublished manuscript, Department of Curriculum Studies, University of Hong Kong.

Yang, S. (2013), *A Combined Approach of CA and CL to Discourse Markers in Chinese College EFL Teacher Talk: A case study*. Unpublished PhD thesis, University of Newcastle.

Young, R. (2003), 'Learning to talk the talk and walk the walk: Interactional competence in academic spoken English', *North Eastern Illinois University Working Papers in Linguistics* 2, 26–44.

Young, R. (2008), *Language and Interaction: An Advanced Resource Book*, London: Routledge.

Zuber-Skerritt, O. (1996), 'Emancipatory action research for organisational change and management development', in O. Zuber-Skerritt (ed.), *New Directions in Action Research*, London: Falmer.

Index